NIETZSCHE'S THOUGHT OF
ETERNAL RETURN

NIETZSCHE'S THOUGHT OF ETERNAL RETURN

Joan Stambaugh

The Johns Hopkins University Press

BALTIMORE AND LONDON

To Glenn

CONTENTS

Prefatory Note   ix

Introduction   xi

  I. *Nietzsche's Understanding of Eternal Return: Eternity*   1
      Explication of the Problem   1
      The Problem of Duration   5
      Eternal Return as the Irreversibility of Time:
        Recurrence as Cycle   8
      Eternal Return as Permanence for Becoming:
        Recurrence as "Being"   13
      Nihilism and the Thought of Eternal Return:
        The Eternal Return of the Same as the
        Most Extreme Form of Nihilism   16
      The Moment   21

  II. *Return: Recurrence of the Same*   29
      The Basic Problem   29
      Three Interpretations   45
        A Fact Belonging to Physics   45
        An Impossibility   51
        A Thought   56

  III. *The Same*   61
      The Problem of the Self   61
      The Self and Eternal Return   69
        The Self: Not a Subject or an Ego   73
        The Will as a Possible Basis for the Self:
          Will and the Will to Power   76

The Self and the Will to Power as Art   82
The Self and the Superman   86
The Will to Power and Eternal Return   94

IV. *Time and Eternal Return*   103
Eternal Return and Traditional Theories of Time   103
The Traditional Relation of Time to Eternity   109
The Significance and Implications of Nietzsche's
    "There Is No End" for a Theory of Time   112
Time   116
    Instantaneity   117
    Irreversibility   117
    Differentiation of the Modes of Past, Present,
        and Future   119
    Neutrality   120
Time and Eternity in the Eternal Return of the
    Same   123

Selected Bibliography   129

Index   131

PREFATORY NOTE

When not otherwise specified, references to Nietzsche's works follow his own internal numerations so that they may be consulted in different English editions or in the German original. In general, Walter Kaufmann's translations have been used with minor alterations. Citations of the untranslated *Nachlass* refer to the German Kröner edition, if they are included there, or to the *Gesammelte Werke*, Gross- und Kleinoktavausgabe, Leipzig. All translations of the *Nachlass* are the author's.

A critical edition of Nietzsche's original texts is being prepared by Giorgio Colli and Mazzino Montinari, Walter de Gruyter, Berlin. This edition will greatly facilitate a unified procedure of quotation. With regard to the question of the "authentic" order of the posthumously published work *The Will to Power*, the chronological grouping in the Schlechta edition is useful for chronological reference. But, since all of the literature on Nietzsche until very recently quoted from Peter Gast and E. Forster-Nietzsche's edition, it seemed advisable to use that edition primarily. The first edition groups the writings thematically, which makes it considerably easier to find particular sections. This grouping is *not* the original grouping, but then an original grouping does not exist. For further, detailed information on this subject, see Nietzsche, *Werke* VIII 2, *Kritische Gesamtausgabe*, edited by von Giorgio Colli and Mazzino Montinari (Berlin: Walter de Gruyter, 1970), and, for English readers, Walter Kaufmann's edition of *The Will to Power* (New York: Random House, 1967).

For the author's earlier, more general treatment of Nietzsche's thought, see *Untersuchungen zum Problem der Zeit bei Nietzsche* (The Hague: Martinus Nijhoff, 1958).

INTRODUCTION

This study attempts to probe into the meaning of Nietzsche's thought of eternal return. Eternal return is probably the most enigmatic concept of Nietzsche's multifaceted philosophy. The thought itself is enigmatic to the Western mind, and the way in which Nietzsche dealt with it might be enigmatic for the Eastern mind as well. Then, Nietzsche's own attitude toward this thought is striking. He does not quite seem to know what to do with it, and yet he cannot leave it alone.

Nietzsche's unusual attitude toward this thought is expressed in his many contradictory statements about it and in the extreme tone of those statements. One might be tempted to say that a philosophy with contradictions is jeopardized by a lack of logical consistency and that such an extreme tone only serves to underscore that lack. However, if one really tries to grapple with the thought of eternal return, one is more likely to see the bottomless difficulties that seem to lie outside the reach and claim of sheer logical consistency.

It is not by chance that Nietzsche constantly refers to the thought of eternal return as "sein schwerster Gedanke," his most weighty thought. *Schwer* means "weighty," "difficult," "hard" (in the sense of "hard to bear"). Thus, the thought of eternal return is *schwer* in the double sense of being extremely difficult and hard to think out, as well as weighty and momentous. Its weightiness or momentousness is not the heaviness of the spirit of gravity (the dwarf in *Zarathustra*, who paradoxically "makes everything too easy for himself"). The weightiness of Nietzsche's thought is the counterpossibility to the attitude that "nothing is true, all is per-

mitted, all is in vain." It is the counterpossibility to meaninglessness and nihilism.

As far as the difficulty of this thought is concerned, it is, like
any truly great thought, hard to think out in all its implications
because it involves the whole. It is also difficult because it has so
little historical precedence in Western philosophy. Even in Eastern philosophy there has been enormous disagreement as to the
meaning and implications of "eternal recurrence."

On the basis of what Nietzsche wrote about his thought of
eternal return, it is not possible to fully comprehend that thought.
There remains something about it, something crucial and essential,
which Nietzsche was unable to communicate. Thus, this study,
having pondered the meaning of Nietzsche's statements, also attempts to inquire into the meaning of eternal return independ-
ently of those statements.

At first glance, the words "eternal return" may not seem to
convey much meaning, at least not an unambiguous meaning. If
one said "eternal recurrence" instead of eternal return and then
proceeded to talk about recurring cycles of nature or the transmigration of souls, the issue would probably be more familiar, although still not clearly meaningful. We are familiar with the idea
of recurrence and transmigration from the early Greeks (particularly the Pythagoreans and Plato) and, above all, from Eastern
thought. It is not an idea which belongs to our own heritage,
however, certainly not to our present heritage.

What is so important about this thought of eternal return?
What prevents it from being a fantastic speculation too remote
from our lives to be of any real concern to us? If we do not blindly
accept Nietzsche's own extreme excitement about it as "the turning point of history" (which it has hardly yet proved to be), we
must ourselves experience the impact of that thought, for, if
Nietzsche's thought is anything at all, it is something which we
must experience.

Nietzsche's account of his discovery of the thought of eternal
return emphasizes the experiential character of that thought.
Stating buffoonishly that the period of gestation for the expression
of the thought of eternal return in *Zarathustra* curiously coincided
with that of the female elephant (a fact, he claims, which any

good Buddhist would immediately recognize), he goes on in a more serious vein.

I would now like to tell you the history of my *Zarathustra*. Its fundamental conception, the idea of *Eternal Recurrence*, the highest formula of affirmation that can ever be attained, belongs to August, 1881. I made a hasty note of it on a sheet of paper, with the post-script: "Six thousand feet beyond man and time." That day I was walking through the woods beside Lake Silvaplana; I halted not far from Surlei, beside a huge, towering pyramidal rock. It was there that the idea came to me. . . . It was on these two roads that all *Zarathustra*, and particularly Zarathustra himself as a type, came to me—perhaps I should rather say—invaded me.[1]

This, in a way, is comparable to Archimedes' experience; while sitting in the bathtub, he suddenly cried out: "Eureka!" But Nietzsche was not sitting in the bathtub; he was walking past the large pyramidal stone near Surlei. And, although the impact of finding came over him just as it came over Archimedes, Nietzsche was not quite sure "what" it was that he had found. The meaning and implications of his thought were more vast and more awesome than those of a principle of physics.

For contemporary man many things have long ceased to be fantastic. The space age has opened up possibilities undreamed of a relatively short time ago. We firmly believe in what one could almost call the "magic" of technology. Technology can do almost anything. It may simply be a matter of time until it can do practically everything. As far as anything "fantastic" or out of the ordinary in the nontechnological sense is concerned, however, we are acutely skeptical. We can fly to the moon, but we are not going to "travel" anywhere in a nonspatial way, in the sense of some transmigration after death. Any kind of "immortality" which we entertain boils down to a kind of prolonged physical survival based on the possibility of transplants and related means of repairing and preserving organisms. This kind of "immortality" amounts to a relative survival of the body.

As far as the other side of our Western dualism, the spirit, is concerned, we are more dubious. A few of us allow for the possibility of an "afterlife" and conceive this as some kind of "state."

[1] *Ecce Homo*, "Thus Spoke Zarathustra," 1.

Many of us stay with the almost overwhelming evidence of the finality of physical death and take this as the absolute end of life. Most of us prefer to postpone thinking about such questions.

Immanuel Kant said that human reason is plagued with questions that it can neither answer nor escape. It cannot answer these questions, because they transcend the faculties of human knowledge. But it cannot get away from them either, because they are inherent in the nature of human reason itself. Kant's conclusion was that questions with regard to the world (the universe), the soul, immortality, and God could never be answered. For instance, the fact that one can logically prove *and* disprove that the world had a beginning meant for Kant that such an undertaking was ultimately fruitless. But perhaps it is not possible to bracket such questions as unanswerable, or even to postpone them indefinitely, which is another, less obvious way of doing the same thing.

We are able to reach out into the realm of space with the astonishing feats of our technology. We cannot do this with "time." Science fiction instinctively experimented with and described both of these possibilities: journeys into space *and* into time (with time machines and such). But we are watching only the "outer" half of these speculations come true. The journeys into time which science fiction writers envisioned have not been taken, essentially because we cannot be *transported, just as we are,* by a machine into another "place" in time.

It was the impact of a new experience of "time," the experience of eternal return, which forced Nietzsche, in spite of all his "sober all-too-sober" naturalistic leanings—sometimes naturalistic to the point of a gross materialism—to plunge again into those questions which Kant had declared unanswerable for the finite human being. Not that anyone's statement that "it cannot be done, it is impossible," would have deterred Nietzsche. But his own distaste for the "religious" and his own mistrust of the nonnatural, let alone the "supranatural," kept him within the boundaries of his own experience. There are no logical constructs in Nietzsche, and there are no religious ones either. Only when his experience was transformed by the thought of eternal return did he enter the realm of those questions.

What, then, is the role of eternal return in Nietzsche's thought? To what kind of questions is it related? Taking any of the major thinkers of the Western philosophical tradition, one can single out their fundamental concepts and see what kind of questions those concepts serve to answer. Since much of Nietzsche's thinking is polemically oriented, many of his ideas are seen as overcoming the related ideas of other thinkers. Thus the Will to Power is Nietzsche's answer to Schopenhauer's Will to Live, and the transvaluation of all values is Nietzsche's answer to Christian morality. But this is not true of the idea of eternal return. The thought of eternal return is not polemical; it is problematical.

What is the problem involved in the thought of eternal return? Is Nietzsche saying primarily that we are born, live, die, and are then reborn? If we are reborn, do we have any consciousness of our previous lives? If so, why are we not aware of those previous lives, since presumably this is not our first life? If there is no memory and continuity of consciousness, in what sense are we the same person at all? If I have no memory of my previous lives, what difference do they make to me, in what sense do they even belong to me?

These are questions with which Eastern thinkers, for whom the idea of rebirth and recurrence is central, have had to cope. Their views on these questions are quite diversified. The Buddhists, for example, do not accept the idea of a substantial soul which wanders from one life to the next. For early Buddhism, man was a collection of components (*skandhas*) that have no intrinsic unity. At death these components are dispersed. What leads to rebirth is the individual's karma—that is, the accumulation of past actions that are not yet "settled." For instance, if a man commits a murder, that deed produces negative karma, and he must be reborn until that accumulated karma has worked itself out. But even "positive" karma accumulated through good deeds leads to rebirth, albeit to a "favorable" rebirth. Buddhism's claim is not that there is an indestructible soul which for the reason of its indestructibility must in some fashion "live on" after death. Rather, deeds and actions (the root meaning of *karma* is "to make or do") cause a certain force to accumulate which must then expend itself and work itself out. It is this unexpended force which leads to rebirth. Ghost stories thrive on a superficial form of the idea, for instance, that the ghost of the past owner of some house to whom misfortune has befallen keeps turning up in that house because he has not found any peace and is not about to let anyone else have any peace either.

Ghost stories aside, the East has seen here a question which the West has largely ignored. Apart from the diversity of views as to the literal or "symbolic" meaning of transmigratory recurrence, a diversity which goes so far as to include the rejection of the whole idea of recurrence, Eastern thinkers have concerned themselves with the question of *finality* (not cessation). And this question of finality is the essential core of the thought which invaded Nietzsche.

The question of finality undercuts the either-or of an "afterlife" or extinction at death. The either-or at stake here is that of an impotent endlessness necessitated by the inability to attain finality or by an attainment of finality which transcends the dichotomy of recurrence and extinction.

These sketchy remarks can do little more than intimate the questions discussed in this study. They should at best point to the kind of questions to which Nietzsche's thought of eternal return is related. Although the affinity of his thought to Eastern ideas is undeniable and some comparisons are therefore inevitable (because the *problem* is the same), such comparisons or references have been kept to a minimum. Nietzsche did not arrive at the thought of eternal return through a study of Eastern thinking, but rather through his own experience. Thus the most appropriate way to understand his thought is to think about it in its own terms, and those are Western terms. There is no reason why Western thinkers should not come to grips with this problem in terms of their own tradition. They might find themselves at the dawn of a new philosophical problem.

Western metaphysics has perhaps exhausted the possibilities of the question, dominant since Plato, of Being and Becoming, of what abides throughout change, or is changeless, and what constantly changes. The question of finality or non-finality, raised in Nietzsche's thought of eternal return, opens up a new dimension of that problem.

NIETZSCHE'S THOUGHT OF
ETERNAL RETURN

*Most godlike things escape knowledge
because of incredulity.*
HERACLITUS

I

NIETZSCHE'S UNDERSTANDING OF ETERNAL RETURN: ETERNITY

EXPLICATION OF THE PROBLEM

Let us take first the word "eternal," which for two reasons is perhaps the most difficult aspect of the thought of eternal return: (1) the concept of eternity is one of the most difficult and misunderstood ideas of Western thought, and (2) Nietzsche's understanding of it seems almost directly opposed to this tradition. "Eternity" is the only traditional concept of metaphysics which Nietzsche did not attack or reject. Every kind of "transcendence"—God, Spirit, Being, the One, the Self, the thing in itself, the historical process—is unmasked by Nietzsche as the inexorable forerunner, even more, as the *cause*, of nihilism. All are more or less concealed forms of a "Beyond"[1] which judges and reduces this world, the only reality the human being has, to something inferior, to something that should not be. All forms of a Beyond are absolute standards that take all "value"[2] out of this world and proclaim it to be nothing. The result of this is nihilism, "the uncanny

[1] *Ein Jenseits.*
[2] The fact that Nietzsche understands the traditional concepts of metaphysics as "values" is in itself a sign of their loss of ontological meaning.

1

guest at the door," now that all the traditional "values" have become shaky and untenable. All value resided in them, and now that they are no longer "real" we suddenly discover the total lack of value in this world. These transcendental concepts have drained our world of value, and we are left with nothing.

Plato[3] was for Nietzsche the culprit who started all this by positing the Idea as that which never changes, which always remains, the standard which the flux of this perishable existence can never reach. For Nietzsche, Christianity, which influenced philosophy through the time of Hegel, was nothing but "Platonism for the people." Thus he described

How the "True World" Finally Became a Fable: The History of an Error

1. The true world—attainable for the sage, the pious, the virtuous man; he lives in it, *he is it*. (The oldest form of the idea, relatively clever, simple, and convincing. A paraphrase of the sentence, "I, Plato, *am* the truth.")

2. The true world—unattainable for now, but promised for the sage, the pious, the virtuous man ("for the sinner who repents"). (Progress of the idea: it becomes more subtle, insidious, incomprehensible—*it becomes female*, it becomes Christian.)

3. The true world—unattainable, undemonstrable, unpromisable; but the very thought of it—a consolation, an obligation, an imperative. (At bottom, the old sun, but seen through fog and skepticism. The idea has become sublime, pale, Nordic, Königsbergian.)

4. The true world—unattainable? At any rate, unattained. And being unattained, also *unknown*. Consequently, not consoling, redeeming, or obligating: how can something unknown obligate us? (Gray morning. The first yawn of reason. The cockcrow of positivism.)

5. The "true" world—an idea which is no longer good for anything, not even obligating—an idea which has become useless and superfluous—*consequently*—a refuted idea: let us abolish it! (Bright day; breakfast; return of *bon sens* and cheerfulness; Plato's embarrassed blush; pandemonium of all free spirits.)

6. The true world—we have abolished. What world has remained? The apparent one perhaps? But no! *With the true world we have also abolished the apparent one.* (Noon; moment of the shortest shadow; end of the longest error; high point of humanity; INCIPIT ZARATHUSTRA.)[4]

[3] Nietzsche's interpretation, of course, oversimplifies Plato, but it touches on something which undeniably emerges in the course of Western philosophy.
[4] *Twilight of the Idols.*

This *pièce de résistance,* in the double sense of that phrase, needs no bulky comment. It is Nietzsche's "history of philosophy" in one page. The question that arises here is: Why did Nietzsche not reject eternity along with the other transcendent or transcendental concepts that belong to it? With what, then, was he left? An eternal *what* or *whom*? If there is no God or Spirit or One or Being to be eternally, what is it that is eternal? The only answer is that Nietzsche had a new and very problematical concept of eternity. What was eternal for him was the return of the Same.

This points toward two possibilities. Nietzsche's eternity is either a kind of totally immanent, endless time—a bad temporal infinity—or it is to be understood only in the light of whatever he meant by the return of the Same.

How has the meaning of eternity been traditionally thought? There are four basic meanings of this word: (1) endless duration; (2) an eternal present (*nunc stans*), a present which never ceases to be present, never becomes past; (3) the simultaneity of all the disparate, disrupted, successive parts of time; and (4) timelessness. The concept which is related to eternity is time, just as Being is related to Becoming, the One to the Many, and so forth. If eternity is to retain a specific meaning which is distinct from these other ideas of the One or of Being, it must be thought in terms of its relation to time. The Western philosophical tradition thinks eternity as some sort of negation, overcoming, prolongation, or gathering together of the successive, passing moments of time. Nietzsche does not.

First of all, for Nietzsche, eternity, the eternal return of the Same, meant "there is no end." To say that there is no end is not the same as to say that the world is endless. What is endless never comes to an end, in the sense that it *endures* on and on without ever encountering anything to stop it. Nietzsche's constant polemic against everything enduring or remaining in the world, against all "Being," excluded the interpretation of "there is no end" as endless duration.

The scope of this fact—that there is no end—cuts across the traditional distinction made between time and eternity, questions them both in a way that nearly reverses their usual meaning, and

3

reaches into a new dimension, which, described generally and in a preliminary fashion, is basically a matter of possibilities of being.

In relation to time, the fact that there is no end means that "Becoming" goes on and on,[5] or, more exactly, that it *happens* again and again.[6] This is a direct contradiction of the idea of time as the prime principle of finitude, as Chronos who devours his own children, as time that inexorably rolls out of the future into the past, drawing everything along with it. This fact cannot be taken to mean that time itself is endless, whereas the time allotted to man is limited. Nietzsche was not speaking of the physicist's time, which belongs to no one, but, as in some sense every philosophical thinker did before him, of time in relation to man. The fact could be simply expressed by saying that in time nothing is ever finished, because time comes, or occurs, again and again. This could be expressed in Hegelian terms by saying that on a certain level anything achieved or completed in time is "superceded" (*aufgehoben*) by the continuing occurrence of time. I cannot eat breakfast "once and for all."

In relation to eternity or any kind of transcendence, to that which is "out of time" (what Nietzsche called the Backworld"), the fact that there is no end means that there is no God as an eternally existing ground of the world, no state of rest, no nirvana, in Schopenhauer's understanding (or misunderstanding) of that word.

To sum up, there is no "once and for all," neither in time nor outside it. This was, in its barest and most neutral form, the thought that "invaded" Nietzsche. The vehemence of this invasion, which Nietzsche describes in *Ecce Homo*, plunged him into an uncharted dimension where the terrible *question* confronted him: What does this mean?

The diversity of Nietzsche's answers, which border on "contradiction," shows the genuineness, but also the initial helplessness, with which he faced this question. He comes up with such completely different interpretations of eternal recurrence as an

---

[5] *Immer weiter.*

[6] *Immer wieder.* This is a genuinely temporal qualification, whereas "on and on" implies a kind of spatial extension.

inexorable natural law, a turning point of history, the highest *spiritual necessity* fatalism, the free creative act of bestowing eternity.

Nietzsche's thought of eternal return does not fit into the classical distinctions of Western philosophy. To further clarify it, it might be advantageous to distinguish it from similar concepts in India. The idea of recurrence is fundamental to almost all forms of Indian thought. Eternal recurrence is something unequivocally fraught with suffering. It is something from which both Brahmanism and early Buddhism (Hinayana)[7] sought to escape, Brahmanism through immersion of the Atman in Brahman, Buddhism through the attainment of nirvana. Nietzsche, however, rejected every kind of striving for release from eternal recurrence as nihilistic. It was precisely eternal recurrence which he wished to *affirm*. He also rejected the interpretation of eternal recurrence as a transmigration of souls, on the ground that it was a "reversed Darwinism."[8] Closely related to this rejection of transmigration was his emphasis on the word "same."

I come again with this sun, with this earth, with this eagle, with this serpent—*not* to a new life, or a better life, or a similar life: I come again eternally to this identical and selfsame life, in its greatest and its smallest, to teach again the eternal return of all things.[9]

No one else, in the West or in the East, has ever made such a statement. Nietzsche's thought is unique.

The Problem of Duration

It has been stated that Nietzsche did not uphold the traditional distinction between time and eternity. This does not mean, however, that he simply *equated* them. The strict "immanence" of Nietzsche's thought does not reduce eternity to the level of time. That element of time which is a "hindrance" to eternity is portrayed in the chapter of *Zarathustra* entitled "Redemption."[10]

---

[7] Mahayana Buddhism and its later form in the Far East do not fall into this category, particularly not the Buddhists who state that there is not a hair's breadth of difference between samsara (the endless recurrence of birth and death) and nirvana (cessation of birth and death).

[8] *Nachlass*, XIV: 125.

[9] *Zarathustra*, "The Convalescent."

[10] The English "redemption" means literally to "buy back." The German *Erlösung* means "release."

Before discussing it, however, an attempt must be made to show that Nietzsche did not conceive of time as a *continuous* flow. If it can be shown that Nietzsche's time was not a continuous process, that it had nothing to do with *duration*, then it will become evident that his concept of eternity is not oriented toward a limited, continuous *stretch* of time overcoming the finitude of this time by endless, continuous prolongation.

This attempt is a difficult one for two reasons. First, Nietzsche never worked out a theory of time, a fact which is interesting and remarkable in itself. Thus there are only fragmentary remarks scattered throughout his writings to indicate his view of it. Second, the few remarks Nietzsche did make about time point toward a conception quite different from most of Western thought, with the possible exception of Leibniz.[11]

The importance of Nietzsche's remarks on time lies in the fact that they contribute something to the problem of "fitting time in" with eternity. This problem can be stated in a somewhat oversimplified fashion as follows: How is eternity to be experienced, how is eternity to "break into" time, if time is conceived as an uninterrupted, continuous, self-contained flow? Those thinkers who experienced eternity as the *nunc stans*, or as the moment, are faced with the extremely difficult problem of relating that *nunc* or moment to the rest of "ordinary" time, which is unquestionably "still there" and flows on. Still more simply stated, the question is: How does one, so to speak, *get out* of this continuous, "horizontally" directed flux? To use the familiar image of the rapidly flowing stream, how can one "stop" that stream, not be inexorably carried along with it into the constantly all-devouring past? Every present immediately becomes past before one can

[11] See his *Monadology*, no. 47: "Thus God alone is the primal unity or the original substance of which all created or derived monads are the products and are generated, so to speak, by continual fulgurations of the Divinity, from moment to moment, limited by the receptivity of the creature, to whom limitation is essential." As stated here, Leibniz's general world view is, of course, quite foreign to Nietzsche's thought. God, primal unity, original simple substance, monads, products, and the Divinity are all "entities" which Nietzsche would reject. But the expressions "continual fulgurations" (continual in contradistinction to continuous, as an adverbial expression, the fact of again and again) and "from moment to moment," have an amazing affinity to Nietzsche's remarks about time.

"catch" it. Even if this should succeed, even if one could experience one moment of time which stood still, what would be the relationship of that "timeless" moment to the rest of time? One cannot *remain* in such a moment; one is thrown back into the constant flux of time. In other words, how is one to think the relation of that one "isolated" moment to the rest of time, especially if there is no static eternity sitting off somewhere apart from time?

The newness of Nietzsche's position with regard to this problem lies in his absolute denial of any duration whatsoever. Duration falls under his Occam's razor, which does not simply slice off universals, but, far more radically, slices off any kind of "substance" whatever, anything that *remains*. The flux of time is in its own way a concealed kind of "substance," for it continuously flows on. The flux itself is constant, continuous. It *always* flows, or "is."

Nietzsche's treatment of this problem is formulated as the relation of "in one moment" to "in every moment." This does *not* coincide with the relation of one moment to the continuous flux of time, for the phrase "in every moment," which occurs frequently and in the most decisive passages, has nothing to do with the whole of time conceived of as continuous flow or even extension (duration). It has a disparate, discrete character.

Nietzsche attacks this interpretation of the opposition of one moment to the rest of time in *The Genealogy of Morals*, where he criticizes Schopenhauer's exaltation of release from the pressure of the ever-driving will.

> How almost pathological is this temporal antithesis between "that moment" and everything else, the "wheel of Ixion," the "hard labor of the will," the vile pressure of the will.[12]

In a polemical fragment which clearly differentiates his thought of eternal return from anything that eternally remains the same, Nietzsche writes:

> Against the value of that which eternally remains the same (Spinoza's naïveté, Descartes' also), the value of the shortest and the most transitory, the seductive flash of gold on the belly of the serpent vita.[13]

[12] *The Genealogy of Morals*, trans. Horace B. Samuel, III: 6.
[13] *The Will to Power*, 577.

7

A few more passages can be quoted to indicate Nietzsche's view of the concepts that belong to the traditional understanding of eternity. The main object of his polemic is substance, which is understood to be anything which constantly remains. The connection here with eternity should be obvious.

The inventive force which devised categories worked in the service of the need for security, for quick intelligibility in the form of signs, sounds, and abbreviations:—"substance," "subject," "object," "being," "becoming," are not matters of metaphysical truth.

If we abandon the acting *subject*, we also abandon the *object* acted upon. Duration, self-identity, being, are inherent neither in what is called subject nor in what is called object. . . . If we abandon the ideas "subject" and "object," then we must also abandon the idea "*substance*"—and consequently its various modifications as well; for instance, "matter," "spirit," and other hypothetical beings, "eternity and immutability of matter," etc.[14]

We have said very little about Nietzsche's actual concept of time. This will become apparent in the subsequent discussions of eternal return itself. We shall treat two possible interpretations of the *structural function* of eternal return. The first interpretation involves an inquiry into that element of time which constitutes a "hindrance" to eternal return, the "it was." The second interpretation leads into the problem of the relation of one moment to every moment, which in turn raises the question of Nietzsche's concept of the Will to Power.

ETERNAL RETURN AS THE IRREVERSIBILITY
OF TIME: RECURRENCE AS CYCLE

If the element of finitude in time is understood as irreversibility, the "eternity" of eternal return consists in making possible a reversal of time. But what does the irreversibility of time mean? And how could eternal return overcome the irreversibility?

Irreversibility is a basic characteristic of time. The past and the future are not indifferent to each other and thus interchangeable, as are the before and behind me of space. What lies in front of and behind me in space constitutes, of course, different directions,

14 *Ibid.*, 513, 552.

but I can turn around and reverse these directions. This is not possible in the case of time. Paradoxically, the irreversibility of time cannot be explained by means of the idea of direction. If I think of irreversibility in terms of growing older, it means: I cannot go backward in time, only forward. If I think of the irreversibility of time in terms of the events approaching me, however, time does not seem to flow forward, but rather past me, going toward the past. Both elements of this paradox have a certain basis in the experience of time. They should not, however, be lumped together and taken to mean that time is reversible. On the contrary, they show that the irreversibility of time means something far more profound than the idea of a direction. Thus eternity as the overcoming of this irreversibility of time cannot be equated with a reversal of the "direction" of time. Furthermore, it is an unquestioned assumption to think that eternity *must* overcome the irreversibility of time. The irreversibility of time could also be thought of as corresponding to something essential and basic to eternity.[15] If this were the case, an attempt to reach eternity by overcoming the irreversibility of "horizontal" time would totally distort and lose the meaning of eternity. Even if eternal recurrence is conceived of as cyclical recurrence (recurrent cycles), it by no means overcomes the "one-wayness" of the cycles. It does not *reverse* the cycles. At best it negates the uniqueness of the process (by repetition), but even this is problematic when one probes into the dimension of "what" returns, of the Same. A cycle is not a finished, completed circle. It has to occur in a forward direction. Only the completed circle is reversible. The "direction" of the circulation of animal bodies is, for example, hardly reversible.

Nietzsche's treatment of the irreversibility of time can be found in the chapter of *Zarathustra* entitled "Redemption."[16] What

[15] See Meister Eckhart (*Deutsche Predigten*, no. 40), who touches on this problem when he says, "The *nunc* [now, eternity] is a taste of time, is a tip [*Spitze*] of time and an end of time." Eternity is thought of here as an extreme possibility of time, a kind of "vertical" culmination of time.

[16] Nietzsche's idea of redemption has nothing to do with Schopenhauer's aim of release from the Will to Live. Nietzsche rejected Schopenhauer's Will to Live, just as in the course of his development he came to reject the whole of Schopenhauer's philosophy with a characteristic vehemence. Nietzsche argues that what is alive cannot will to live, for it is already alive. What is not alive, cannot will. Nietzsche saw Schopenhauer's Will to Live as a form of a will for duration (substance).

Nietzsche means by "redemption" has its roots in the relation of the will to time. This relation has always been characterized by *revenge*.

By the rather unexpected word "revenge," Nietzsche does not simply mean a subjective, "human" emotion. The latter would correspond to Nietzsche's concept of *ressentiment*. Revenge is an *ontological* concept, which means it is a possibility—according to Nietzsche, *the* exclusively dominating actuality of Life itself up to now.[17]

"It was"—That is the name of the will's gnashing of teeth and most secret melancholy. Powerless against what has been done, he is an angry spectator of all that is past. The will cannot will backwards; and that he cannot break time and time's covetousness, that is the will's loneliest melancholy. . . . That time does not run backwards, that is his wrath; . . . and on all who can suffer he wreaks revenge for his inability to go backwards. This, indeed, this alone, is what *revenge* is: the will's revulsion[18] against time and its "it was."[19]

Revenge is the will's revulsion against time and its "it was." The will as revulsion is the counterpart of the Will to Power; it is powerless against what has been done. The will as revulsion cannot go backward; it cannot break time and time's desire. Revulsion is precisely the will that wills, that *must* will, against the irreversibility of time.

The will that is the Will to Power must will something far higher than a reconciliation with time. Nietzsche asked: How does this come about? Who taught the will to will backward?

The redemption of the past comes about when every "it was" is transformed into "thus I willed it." Does this mean that the will is confronted with the "it was" as something irrevocable and unalterable, something it can no longer do anything about, and then says to itself: That is exactly what I willed? Is not this retroactive affirmation a kind of desperate heroism on the part of the will? Can it really redeem the past? Would it not, on the contrary, defeat itself, give up in a fury of impotence, and sing the "fable

[17] See *Zarathustra*, II, "Redemption": "The spirit of revenge, my friends, that has hitherto been man's best contemplation [*Nachdenken*]."
[18] *Gegen-Wille*, a will exclusively oriented *against* something.
[19] *Zarathustra*, II, "Redemption."

of madness"[20]—that is, renounce all willing? And how would all of this reverse time?

The will that is the Will to Power does not simply say: "Thus I willed it." It also says: "Thus do I will it, thus shall I will it!" The *whole* of time is at stake here. The past, which is to be redeemed somehow, contains time as a whole within itself. But time as a whole is eternal return.

The most obvious interpretation of reconciliation with time as a whole would be that the past is affirmed; then time's endless repetition, its coming again and again, would also be affirmed. However, this interpretation equates the "it was" with some past event and approaches what Nietzsche calls "Turkish fatalism," when man stands before the future with folded hands.[21] The "it was" is not something which was once there in the past and is now causing the will to stumble because it wants to will forward. The "it was" is a fragment, so to speak, a piece of crystallized, rigidified time, until the creating will says to it: "But thus I willed it!"

One must consider Nietzsche's exact mode of expression here. He does not speak of redemption from *time*, but rather of redemption from *revenge*. What is related to time is not redemption, not even reconciliation. "The will that is the Will to Power must will something far higher than reconciliation."

---

[20] *Ibid.*

[21] *The Wanderer and His Shadow*, 61: "*Turkish fatalism.* Turkish fatalism contains the fundamental error of placing man and fate opposite each other like two separate things: Man, it says, can strive against fate, can try to defeat it, but in the end it always remains the winner, for which reason the smartest thing to do is to give up or live just any way at all. The truth is that every man himself is a piece of fate; when he thinks he is striving against fate in the way described, fate is being realized here, too; the struggle is imaginary, but so is resignation to fate; all these imaginary ideas are included in fate. The fear which most people have of the doctrine of determinism of the will is precisely the fear of this Turkish fatalism. They think man will give up weakly and stand before the future with folded hands because he cannot change anything about it; or else he will give free rein to his total caprice because even this cannot make what is once determined still worse. The follies of man are just as much a part of fate as his cleverness: this fear of the belief in fate is also fate. You yourself, poor frightened man, are the invincible Moira reigning far above the gods; for everything which comes you are blessing or curse and in any case the bonds in which the strongest man lies. In you the whole future of the human world is predetermined; it will not help you if you are terrified of yourself" (author's translation).

Revenge is the will's revulsion against time and its "it was." Revenge seeks for what is responsible, for what has robbed existence of its innocence.[22] Redemption from revenge consists in winning back the "innocence of becoming."[23]

The instinct of revenge looks for a ground,[24] a reason for its suffering, suffering in the broadest sense of undergoing something. Suffering in this sense is an "ontological" concept, not a pessimistic one governed by wishful thinking[25] (I suffer; the world is "bad" [pessimus]; I wish it were otherwise; it ought to be otherwise). The Will to Power is not Being, not Becoming, but pathos.[26] This cause or reason can lie only in the past, in the "it was." Thus the "it was" becomes the cause for the present, which, however, then loses its true character of presence and becomes a mere consequence, a powerless continuance of the past. The present is irrevocably lost before it can even begin to be, for as a consequence (effect) it can never get behind its cause, which must always be "before" it. Given this meaning of irreversibility, it is absolutely impossible for the will to will backward. The meaning of the "it was," of the past in general, lies not in losing the present through its flowing by into the past. Rather, the "it was" obstructs every possibility of the occurrence of any real present. The meaning of finitude which is implicit here is not that everything passes away, but that everything is rigidified in the past—more exactly, that everything has always already become rigidified because of the unconditioned, inexorable priority of the cause.

Thus eternal return is truly meaningless, for it occurs on the temporal foundation of the "it was," of the "always-already-there." Recurrence is not only a superfluous repetition, it is nihilistic—that is, any possible originality of occurring, anything new whatsoever, is annihilated by the foundation of the "it was." In this case re-

---

[22] The Will to Power, 765.

[23] A phrase which recurs often in Nietzsche's late sketches.

[24] See Nachlass, XII: 300: "The belief in cause and effect has its place in the strongest of the instincts: in the instinct of revenge."

[25] Wünschbarkeit. This is a basic idea in Nietzsche's thought. Briefly, it means the unsuccessful, venomous attempt to think things as they ought to have been, not as they "are."

[26] The Will to Power, 635.

currence is not a hindrance to Life[27]—to the Will to Power. Rather, the "it was" is a hindrance to eternal return.

Zarathustra understands himself as the advocate and justifier of all finitude.[28] What he means by finitude is neither the passing away of the present into the past nor the self-rigidifying of the past. The attitude which Nietzsche opposes to revenge is that of justice, which "hinders rigidification through constant change."[29]

He who justifies finitude is he who "justifies the future and redeems the past, for he wants to perish through the present."[30] What does this mean, to perish[31] through the present, if the past is redeemed? If the past is redeemed, perishing can no longer be thought of as a sinking back into the past, for the past is "redeemed"—that is, *released* and no longer attainable as something rigidified. Perishing is thus not a return to the "it was." It occurs through the present. Here Nietzsche thinks of irreversibility not as the impossibility of going back to the past, but as letting the present *end* (in and through the present).

Eternal Return as Permanence for Becoming: Recurrence as "Being"

If finitude is understood to mean impermanence, eternal return is that which gives permanence to Becoming, in the sense that the Same recurs again and again, thus constituting a kind of interrupted, periodically recurring duration. The passage that seems to support this interpretation is found in the *Will to Power* (617): "*That everything recurs,* is the closest approach of a world of Becoming to a world of Being."

Because there is nothing permanent in the world, the only possibility of having something endure is to have it perish, but come again.[32] In relation to the Will to Power, eternal return thus constitutes the conditions for increasing that Will to Power. If the

---

[27] *Nachlass*, XII: 369.
[28] *Vergänglichkeit*.
[29] *Human, All-Too-Human*, I: 637.
[30] Preface to *Zarathustra*.
[31] *Zugrundegehen*; literally, "to go to the ground."
[32] Instead of saying to the moment, "Tarry awhile, you are so beautiful" (as Faust did), Nietzsche says, "Go, but come back."

13

Will to Power is a continuous self-increasing, a will to be *more*,[33] then it needs something stable, something which constantly remains to be overcome and thus gives rise to more. Otherwise the Will to Power would simply be a chaotic flux.

This interpretation of eternal return depends entirely on the interpretation of the Will to Power. It might therefore be best to say something about the Will to Power at this point. If Nietzsche's idea of recurrence has mostly been met with a lack of understanding and a shrug of the shoulders, his idea of the Will to Power has been met with all too much *mis*understanding. The Will to Power is not "political." It is, according to Nietzsche, the essence of Life. *"This world is the Will to Power—and nothing else! And even you yourselves are this Will to Power—and nothing else!"* [34]

The Will to Power is Nietzsche's long thought-out answer to Schopenhauer's Will to Live; it has nothing to do with the will for self-preservation. The first problem about the concept is what Nietzsche meant by the word "power." The second problem is the relation of the Will to Power to eternal return.

The Will to Power and eternal return have been understood by some interpreters of Nietzsche as mutually exclusive opposites. The Will to Power strives for increase, for more, while eternal recurrence brings back the *Same*, thus excluding any possibility of increase or change.

Heidegger sees eternal return as the existence, Will to Power as the essence, of things, and thus he places Nietzsche within the framework of metaphysics as its last figure. Heidegger often interprets the Will to Power as the Will to Will. This would bring the Will to Power quite close to Schopenhauer's Will. Nietzsche, however, never really got into Schopenhauer's incredible metaphysical brew of blind, striving Will, Platonic Ideas, Kantianism, and a vague Indian ontology. Unfortunately, Heidegger's view is far too comprehensive to go into here, for it involves a complete treatment of the history of "metaphysics."

Nietzsche distinguishes his concept of the Will to Power from mere Becoming in the sense of an unceasing, chaotic flux. Most

---

[33] *Nachlass*, XIV: 508.
[34] *The Will to Power*, 1067.

of his later writings are relentlessly concerned with distinguishing the Will to Power from Schopenhauer's insatiable, blind Will, a will which can never find rest or appeasement, because it is in itself a lack. Against Schopenhauer, Nietzsche places the *fullness* and superabundance of the Will to Power. If *Will* and *Power* in the Will to Power are not simply two unrelated words, and if Power is not something *after* which the Will *strives*, then the Will to Power *exists in the form of* Power, is empowering. The "to" in the Will to Power does not refer to something *outside* the Will, something which it lacks and is striving to attain. It refers to what is "willed" and thus *actualized* in active affirmation. *This* Will to Power needs no "Being" to guarantee it permanence. The Will to Power has nothing to do with permanence or continuance. It has to do with a continual, ever-increasing affirmation. The link between the Will to Power and eternal return lies in the word "continual." Both the Will to Power and eternal return have to do with continual activity.

Nietzsche states that the Will to Power is a Will to More.[35] If this More were understood quantitatively as an on and on, as a guarantee of permanence, then eternal recurrence would be the eternity which the Will to Power wills as its own continuance. This quantitative More would *not* be an increase, however, but preservation, the preservation against which so much of Nietzsche's polemic is directed. The Will to More would be what he calls the demand for a world of constancy. When the living being can no longer will *more*, can no longer increase, it *eo ipso* becomes *less*. There is no possibility of maintaining a stable state of being in the world of the Will to Power, because this stable state is in itself a decline measured against the ever-increasing, power-full nature of the world.

The More, the increase, does not come about as a frantic attempt to gather up everything and preserve it, which would mean "that Life had *withdrawn* from the Whole and was basking luxuriously in trivia."[36] Nietzsche thinks increase and power as a kind of giving back, an act of return.

[35] *Nachlass*, XIV: 508.
[36] *Letters*, I: 54.

15

You force all things to and into yourself that they may flow back out of your well as the gifts of your love. . . . Power is she, this new virtue; a dominant thought is she, and around her a wise soul: a golden sun, and around it the serpent of knowledge.[37]

The images which Nietzsche uses here to describe the virtue called power are those he uses in the Prologue to *Zarathustra* to describe eternal return. Power is also defined here as "dominant thought," which points to the thought of thoughts, the thought of eternal return. This does not mean that the Will to Power and eternal return are the "same." They are, however, inseparable.

The relation of increase (Will to Power) to the Same (eternal return) is certainly difficult to fathom, but it is by no means self-contradictory. It points toward a dimension in which the More becomes an assimilating power,[38] a dimension which makes possible eternal return as *Seligpreisung* ("intense, joyful affirmation"), *sub specie aeterni*.[39] Life is a source of Joy.[40] Joy is a plus-feeling of Power,[41] a symptom of the feeling of attained power.[42] The Will to More lies in the very essence of Joy.[43] Joy, however, "wants itself, wants eternity, wants recurrence, wants all things eternally like itself."[44] Joy does not, like woe, want heirs, children; joy is "more terrible, more mysterious than all woe; it wants *itself*, it bites into *itself*, the ring's will strives in it."[45] "For every ring strives (*ringt*) and turns to reach itself again."[46]

NIHILISM AND THE THOUGHT OF ETERNAL RETURN: THE ETERNAL RETURN OF THE SAME AS THE MOST EXTREME FORM OF NIHILISM

With the title "The Crisis: Nihilism and the Thought of Eternal Return,"[47] Nietzsche explicitly asks about the *meaning* of his

[37] *Zarathustra*, I, "The Bestowing Virtue."
[38] *Gleichen* in the verbal sense, roughly equivalent to as*simil*ating. But *simil* does not preserve the ambiguity of the German *gleich*.
[39] *Nachlass*, XIV: 301. It is *Aeterni*, not *aeternitatis*, as one might expect.
[40] *Zarathustra*, II, "On the Rabble."
[41] *The Will to Power*, 699.
[42] *Ibid.*, 688.
[43] *Ibid.*, 695.
[44] *Zarathustra*, IV, "The Drunken Song." *Alles-sich-ewig-gleich.*
[45] *Ibid.*
[46] *Zarathustra*, II, "On the Virtuous."
[47] Crisis in the full meaning of κρίνειν, de-cido, separate.

thought of return. The crisis occurs as the confrontation of two
extreme positions, of two extreme possibilities of this thought. It
is either (1) the most extreme form of nihilism (the European form
of Buddhism) or (2) the self-attainment of the Same in every
moment. The crisis separates the two meanings of eternal return
and raises the question: Which of these meanings shall man
actualize?

1. Duration with an "in vain," without goal or purpose, is a most
   paralyzing thought. . . . Let us think this thought in its most terrible form: existence, as it is, without meaning or aim, but inevitably recurring, without a finale, into nothingness: "the eternal
   recurrence." This is the most extreme form of nihilism: nothingness (meaninglessness) eternally! European form of Buddhism.
2. There one understands that what is being aimed at here is the
   opposite of pantheism: for "everything perfect, divine, eternal" also
   constrains to a belief in "eternal recurrence." Question: Has this
   pantheistic affirmation of all things also been made impossible by
   morality? At bottom, only the moral god has been overcome. Is
   there any sense in thinking a god "beyond Good and Evil"? Would
   pantheism in *this* sense be possible? Can we remove the idea of
   purpose from the process and *still* affirm the process?—That would
   be the case if something within that process were *attained* in every
   moment—and always the Same. . . . *Every fundamental characteristic*[48] which underlies every event, which expresses itself in
   every event, would have to drive the individual to affirm triumphantly every moment of existence in general, if the individual
   experienced it as *his* fundamental characteristic.[49]

1. Nietzsche's thought of eternal return is described here in a
form in which he himself experienced it with horror: existence, just
as it is, without meaning and without purpose, inevitably recurring without a finale into nothingness. Nietzsche understood this
form of his thought to be the European form of Buddhism. A few
remarks might be made about the relationship of Nietzsche's
thought of eternal return in this form of the most extreme nihilism
to corresponding ideas in Buddhism. Nietzsche's understanding of
Buddhism is not crucial here, since for the most part he equated
Buddhism with his conception of Christianity as a religion of ex-

---

[48] *Grundcharakterzug.*
[49] *The Will to Power*, 55.

17

haustion and negation; what is crucial is the extent of the affinities to, and differences from, Buddhism in Nietzsche's thought. First of all, it must be emphasized that Nietzsche's thought of eternal return does not coincide with the samsara (cycle of birth and death) of Buddhism, just as it does not coincide with the few related Western ideas. It is hardly a matter of chance, though, and it is certainly worthy of thought that this thought, the origins of which are supposed to be primarily Indian, appeared for the first time and with such tremendous emphasis to Nietzsche.

The affinities of Nietzsche's thought in general, not just the thought of eternal return, to other ideas of Buddhism, are astonishing. The denial of substance, of the soul, of the universal, and of duration; an emphasis on suffering in the sense of ontological restlessness, on the absolute order of the world ("causality": not in the sense of efficient cause or even of the other Aristotelian causes, but in the sense of dependent origination, of things arising together, of the absolute momentariness of the Will to Power[50])— all are present in Nietzsche and in Buddhism. Other elements, too, which cannot be formulated as "doctrines"—for example, the rejection of theoretical knowledge as its own end, or the manner of communication together with the question of what can be communicated—bring Nietzsche very close to Buddhism. But here the affinity stops. Nietzsche's thought that exactly the Same comes again and again—Same is here understood to be some kind of *content*, an important point to be dealt with later—is not common to Buddhism or any other idea in India or the West.

It is Nietzsche's absolute *affirmation* of recurrence which sets his thought apart from the related Indian idea. But the question is: Just *what* is it about recurrence that Nietzsche affirms? Existence, just as it is, inevitably recurring without a finale into nothingness is the thought of eternal return in its *most terrible form*. Perhaps Nietzsche did think a finale to this inevitably recurring existence, and in such a way that inevitable recurrence would not reach the real dimension of the thought of eternal return. What kind of finale this might be is, of course, highly problematical. It could not end in nothingness. It would hardly be meaningful, let alone

[50] *Nachlass*, XIII: 62, 65.

inevitable, if it were not conceived of as the denial of necessarily recurring existence, as the positing of an end to this existence.

2. The other extreme possibility of the thought of eternal return strives for the opposite of traditional pantheism. Actually, it strives for a new, nonstatic, nonmoralistic pantheism. Not only does eternally recurring nothingness bring us to a belief in eternal recurrence; the statement "everything is perfect, divine, eternal" does so too.

• What does Nietzsche mean here by "the opposite of pantheism"? Pantheism means "God is (in) everything." This "god" is a moral god—more abstractly expressed, the idea of a purpose in the world process, for the sake of which everything ultimately occurs. In accordance with the world itself as his point of departure, Nietzsche's opposite kind of pantheism could be defined thus: "Everything is godlike." The "opposition" in this concept of pantheism lies not in the simple exchange of nothing for all as God (God is all things, God is nothing), but rather in what is meant by "God." An understanding of what Nietzsche means by "God" (after the death of God [of "Platonism"]) is essential and prerequisite to an understanding of what he means by "all things."

The few passages in Nietzsche's writings where he speaks of God without polemic and caricature point to a relation of God to Power.

The only possibility of maintaining a meaning for the concept "God" would be: God *not* as driving force, but God as maximum state, as an epoch.[51]

"God" as moment of culmination: existence an external deifying and undeifying[52]—But no culmination of value in this, rather a culmination of Power.[53]

God—the highest Power—that is enough! From this follows *everything*, from it follows—"the world"![54]

What happens to "all things" when they are thought of together with the godlike as Power? Power is nothing persisting, en-

---

[51] *The Will to Power*, 639; author's translation.
[52] *Vergottung und Entgottung* ("deifying and undeifying").
[53] *The Will to Power*, 712; author's translation.
[54] *Ibid.*, 1037.

during. It is a More, a growing tension which differs from endless Becoming. How could this More embrace all things so that one could say "all is godlike"? Inclusion is obviously out of place here. Power as More is not a universal, general whole which subsumes and includes the sum of manifold things in the world. It is not a general whole which is always present to guarantee inclusion.[55]

If Power were a universal generic whole present at all times, it would be, according to Nietzsche, exactly that which makes existence into a monstrosity. Correspondingly, eternity as the "life-dimension" of this Power (its manner of being) would again be a general whole, an "always." Time would merely be the dissected parts of this whole and would have no reality of its own whatsoever. To give to time a reality of its own is not to absolutize or glorify it, but to save it from being a superfluous image of an irrevocable fragmenting of the "true Whole."

Another possibility inherent in the idea of eternity as a general whole would be the absolute mutual exclusion of time and eternity. Strictly speaking, however, it is not possible to describe the relation of time to eternity as a contradiction, if a contradiction consists of two mutually exclusive elements "beside" each other. First of all, there is the difficulty that the principle of contradiction is itself partly defined in terms of time (the same attribute cannot *at the same time* belong and not belong to the same subject in the same respect). It is therefore a questionable undertaking to apply the principle of contradiction to an element which defines it. The more important, essential difficulty, however, lies in the nature of time itself. If time is thought as that which does not remain, and not as a continuous form of finitude, it does not persist in such a manner as to be the opposite of anything. Time can never be the opposite or the contradiction of eternity. One might say that it "relates" to eternity, which is, strictly speaking, the only thing to which it can relate. If there is something "temporal" about eternity (otherwise one might equally well or even better speak of the One, of Being, or of the Absolute, all of which

---

[55] Not even as a whole of Force. See *ibid.*, 331: "It seems to me of the utmost importance that we should rid ourselves of the notion of *the* Whole, of an entity, and of any kind of power or force of the Unconditioned.... *There is no 'All,'* there *is no* great sensorium or inventarium or force-magazine."

have no relation to time, but rather exclude it), it cannot have anything "beside" it. As opposed to the traditional One or Absolute, which can have nothing beside it for the reason that there would then be *two* Absolutes, two Ones, and hence none at all, eternity has no relation to extension, to "space," at all, space in its broadest possible meaning of having something "next to" it,[56] whether this "next to" be understood as coexistence or dissection or as a manifold which is to be worked over into moments and negated,[57] or even as the total "next to" of a succession. The "absolute" quality of eternity is not an unapproachable freedom (*absolute*), it is rather a free*ing* (*ab-solvere*).

Nietzsche conceives of the extreme opposite of the most extreme form of nihilism in such a way that something is attained within the process at each moment of the process, and the something is always the Same. One can see that Nietzsche means something other than nihilism ("something" is "attained"), but that he excludes teleology. Because each moment cuts across, so to speak, the teleological kind of process, no moment is *for the sake* of another.

THE MOMENT

The moment plays an important part in Nietzsche's thought. It is strongly emphasized in the relation of midday to eternity. The expression "midday and eternity" is found throughout Nietzsche's *Nachlass* plans and sketches, as a title or simply as a phrase without any further comment. The phrase "in every moment" receives less emphasis by itself, but it appears again and again in various contexts.

The moment is familiar to us from the philosophical tradition, although its relation to midday places it in a new light. The first thinker to ask explicitly about the moment was Plato.

But there is no time during which a thing can be at once neither in motion nor at rest. On the other hand it does not change without making a transition. When does it make the transition, then? Not

[56] Kant's space as the form of coexistence; see his *Critique of Pure Reason* (New York: Anchor Books, 1966), A23, B38.
[57] Hegel's *Aufgehoben*.

21

while it is at rest or while it is in motion, or while it is occupying time. Consequently, the time at which it will be when it makes the transition must be that strange thing, the instant. The word "instant" appears to mean something such that *from it* a thing passes to one or the other of the two conditions. There is no transition *from* a state of rest so long as the thing is still at rest, nor *from* motion so long as it is still in motion, but this strange thing, the instant, is situated between the motion and the rest; it occupies no time at all, and the transition of the moving thing to the state of rest, or of the stationary thing to being in motion, takes place *to* and *from* the instant. Accordingly, the one, since it is both at rest and in motion, must pass from the one condition to the other—only so can it do both things—and when it passes, it makes the transition instantaneously; it occupies no time in making it and at that moment it cannot be either in motion or at rest.[58]

The word "instant" ($\varepsilon\xi\alpha i\varphi\nu\eta s$) means literally "out of the unseen," suddenly, unexpectedly. Plato calls it a strange thing. It is the moment of transition, and yet it itself occupies no time at all. Transition in the instant is instantaneous.

Aristotle speaks of the now ($\nu\upsilon\nu$), not of the instant, but his statements are very close to those of Plato. For Aristotle, too, the now is not a part of time.

Time, on the other hand, is not held to be made up of "nows."
The "now" is in one sense the same, in another it is not the same. In so far as it is in succession, it is different (which is just what its being now was supposed to mean), but its substratum is an identity.

Time, then, also is both made continuous by the "now" and divided at it. . . . In so far then as the "now" is a boundary, it is not time.[59]

Aristotle shares Plato's attitude toward the strange now or instant and elucidates its nature with the help of dialectical statements. The now both divides time and makes it continuous, and yet it is not a part of time. These statements of Plato and Aristotle on the nature of the instant have remained definitive for the problem ever since. With the exception of an emphasis on the subjective nature of time beginning with Augustine, nothing basic has changed in the manner in which time and the instant are treated.

---

[58] Plato, *Parmenides*, 156d; Cornford's translation, with revisions by author.
[59] Aristotle, *Physics*, bk. 4, chap. 10; McKeon's translation.

Nietzsche's own concept of the instant or moment does not radically depart from the traditional concept. He, too, emphasizes its unique and enigmatic character. Two fragments from the *Nachlass* might serve as illustrations. Both are absolutely incompatible with the traditional interpretations of (1) the superman and (2) eternal recurrence.

Goal: to *attain* the superman for one moment. *For this* I suffer everything![60]

The moment is immortal in which I produced return. For the sake of this moment I *bear* return.[61]

These fragments emphasize the tremendous power of the moment, the unbearableness of its intensity. In the first fragment, if the superman is something to be attained for one moment, he or it is obviously not the product of a supervised pseudo-Darwinian evolution.[62] Actually, the only possible interpretation of the superman in this fragment would be that it is in some sense a state of being or an experience of a higher reality.

In the second fragment, if (eternal) return is something which Nietzsche himself *produced* in an immortal moment, all the connotations of determined, inexorable cycles of recurring existence are simply out of place. Anything which Nietzsche could *produce* in an immortal moment must be some sort of inner reality. He would hardly have designated himself an Indian Brahman-god breathing the world out of himself and then breathing it back in after innumerable kalpas (immense periods of time).

A third fragment, also from the *Nachlass*, closely resembles the first two: "Light, peace, *no exaggerated* longing is happiness in the eternalized moment rightly applied."[63] The first question that arises here is what Nietzsche could have meant by "rightly applying" the eternalized moment. How can a moment be "applied"? Surely not in the customary sense of some kind of "use." Perhaps Nietzsche was referring to a unique experiencing of that eternalized

[60] *Nachlass*, XIV: 306.
[61] *Ibid.*, XII: 371.
[62] A current interpretation of Nietzsche's hopes for the superman, for which there is actually some basis in Nietzsche's writings.
[63] *Nachlass*, XIV: 286.

moment. The experience is characterized by light, peace, happiness, and a lack of exaggerated longing. This is far removed from the Nietzsche who harshly attacked the present state of nearly everything. It points toward the direction in which Nietzsche might have gone had he not entered intellectual darkness; certainly he knew it, if only in brief, isolated moments.

One last fragment should be discussed here before we go on to consider the meaning of the phrase "in every moment" and of the relationship between the moment and "in every moment."

The first question is by no means whether we are content with ourselves, but whether we are content with anything at all. If we affirm one single moment, we thus affirm not only ourselves, but all existence. For nothing is self-sufficient, neither in us nor in things, and if our soul has trembled with happiness and sounded like a harpstring just once, all eternity was needed to produce this one event—and in this single moment of affirmation, all eternity was called good, redeemed, justified, and affirmed.[64]

There is an intimate connection between the moment, ourselves, and all existence. We and all existing things are not just accidentally existing in the moment. Rather, we are so bound up with the moment that, if we affirm it, we affirm the whole of existence. How can one affirmative moment be sufficient to justify and affirm the whole of existence and, implicitly, the whole of "time," all the "rest" of time? Could not the ponderous remainder of existence, all the other "negative" or even terrible experiences, far outweigh a single moment, so that we would perhaps even forget it in our despair? Is not the moment at best an isolated, trumped-up, overwrought experience of the privileged mad few, clung to with an insistent, tenacious will for special ecstasy? Perhaps precisely because nothing is self-sufficient, neither in ourselves nor in things, we could never maintain the integrity of that moment, its perfect affirmative intactness. How is the statement "All eternity was needed to produce that event" to be understood? Here one is faced with the seeming paradox of eternity producing a moment in time. This rules out the possible interpretation of eternity as endlessness or even as the whole of durational time, for it is very

[64] *The Will to Power*, 1032.

difficult to see how a moment in time could be produced by the whole of time when that whole of time had not yet occurred. All future time after the moment would be excluded, thus seriously jeopardizing the integrity of eternity. We shall leave this difficult question for a later chapter.

The phrase "in every moment" has less of a basis in philosophical tradition than does Nietzsche's concept of the moment. One is tempted to ask what Nietzsche meant by this phrase and why he placed such emphasis on it. Why "in *every* moment"? Is this not an impossible claim, to affirm existence in every moment? What is the relation of the moment to the "in every moment"? Is the moment the timeless *nunc stans* of eternity and the "in every moment" the unattainable imperative of having the *nunc stans* in every moment, of having every moment be a *nunc stans?* Or, does not the moment as *nunc stans* exclude all other moments, all other "time"? The moment and the "in every moment" seem to be incompatible. If the moment is a unique state, then the "in every moment" lies outside that state as the endless flux of time which cannot be contracted into a moment, but rather tries to pull the moment along with it and to annihilate its standing by forcing it to flow on.

The phrase "in every moment" is exactly what Nietzsche set against duration with an "in vain" as the most paralyzing thought in the passage cited previously. If something were attained within the world process in every moment and if the individual were to experience this as *his* own being, he could triumphantly affirm all existence in every moment. The phrase "in every moment" emphasizes the absolute lack of any kind of duration in the universe:

But then it [the individual] discovers that it is itself something changing and has a changing taste. It discovers in its freedom the mystery that there is no individual, that in the smallest moment it is something other than in the next moment. . . . the *infinitely small moment* is the higher reality and truth is a lightning flash out of the eternal flux.[65]

[65] *Nachlass*, XII: 45.

Small wonder that Nietzsche felt a kinship with Heraclitus. Not only does the "in every moment" preclude any duration; it also precludes any kind of teleology. No moment exists for the sake of another. Nothing is put off or deferred for the sake of some future time which may never be realized. This is perhaps the most basic meaning of Nietzsche's phrase. The present moment is to be lived fully and at once. It is never to be postponed or even neglected for some reminiscence of the past. Either one lives in the present or one does not live at all.

In contrast to this possibility, eternal recurrence in the paralyzing form of duration determines that which comes again, the Same, as content. In statically persisting duration, it is impossible to think of a real coming-again as the event of time itself, because time conceived of as duration has always already happened, it is already "over" and thus determined. If this duration is thought of as being cyclical, an idea with many unsolved, *unasked* difficulties (for example, what makes this duration turn back on itself to form a cycle instead of simply persisting on linearly?), the meaning of the Same changes from that of remaining like itself to that of the Same coming again and again. Whereas the meaning of a unique process lies in the goal or end of that process, the meaning of a recurring process becomes relegated, transferred, strangely enough, to *what* recurs. In a determined series of recurring events the "when" of an event is already established. The "what" is not totally predictable, because the element of repetition enforces and strengthens the effect of the event. To go to the dentist for the tenth time this year is different from going for the first time. It is true that one knows more what to expect the tenth time, but one has perhaps also acquired a keener imagination of possible experiences from those nine other visits. Nietzsche was aware of these implications.

Let us see how the *thought* that *something repeats itself* has had an effect up to now. (The year, for example, or periodic illnesses, waking and sleeping, etc.) If cyclical repetition is even a probability or a possibility, even the *thought of a possibility* can terrify and transform us, not only feelings or definite expectations! Think of the effect of the *possibility* of eternal damnation![66]

[66] *Ibid.*, 63.

An intensified inquiry into the structure of return and of recurrence may shed some light on the problem of the moment. It should be pointed out here that, apart from his emphasis on the presence of the moment, Nietzsche's secondary emphasis with regard to eternal recurrence is on the future, on the anticipatory experience of recurrence, not on the past.

II

RETURN:
RECURRENCE OF
THE SAME

The Basic Problem

Discussion of the word "eternal" in Nietzsche's thought of eternal return of the Same inevitably brings us into the thought itself in its entirety. It is impossible to speak of "eternal" without reference to its "structure" (return) or to its even more problematic "what." Focusing on return and recurrence, this chapter will attempt to penetrate somewhat deeper into Nietzsche's thought of thoughts.

Up to now, the expressions "return" and "recurrence" have been used more or less interchangeably, as Nietzsche himself used them.[1] We have used the word "recurrence" perhaps more frequently in dealing with cycles as such because the word "return" seems at first too general to express Nietzsche's basic idea of constant coming again and again. Nietzsche himself, however, uses both words, and, without going into a statistical frenzy, it can be stated that he uses *return* in most of the "crucial" passages. A clear-cut distinction between recurrence and return will not, how-

---

[1] *Wiederkunft* as "return"; *Wiederkehr* as "recurrence."

ever, "solve the problem," for Nietzsche made no systematic use of such a distinction.

It is significant that Nietzsche almost never used the word "repetition" (*Wiederholung*). This would have been a more familiar and less ambiguous expression, had he meant exclusively the exact repetition of all things (including man) in a determined series.

Wiederkehr ("recurrence") and *Wiederkunft* ("return") are very close in meaning. They share, along with *Wiederholung* ("repetition") , the prefix *Wieder* (Latin, *re*), which means both "again" and "back." Etymologically, the "turn" of *return* lies in the German *Wieder*kehr. Still, *recurrence* comes closer to *Wiederkehr* in actual usage, as does *return* to *Wiederkunft*.

A basic distinction between *Wiederkehr* and *Wiederkunft*, more sharply drawn in English than in German, is that what *recurs* is an event, something which has previously occurred. What *returns* might be anything, including a person, which goes back to where it was. A recurrence is something which has *run through* its course and occurs again. A return implies a turning about and going back to an original place or state. A person cannot "recur" home; an event cannot "return," in the sense of going back to its original state. *Return* emphasizes a going back, a *completion* of movement. *Recurrence* emphasizes *another* occurrence or beginning of a movement. Thus *recurrence* is closer in meaning to *repetition* than is *return*.

In the prefix *Wieder* ("again"), which is related to *Wider* ("against"), there is a movement of renewal which presupposes having come back to some original place or state. This prefix, common to both of Nietzsche's expressions, is basic, for it incorporates and guarantees the meaning "again and again."

From these considerations it becomes obvious that, apart from inextricably involving the word "eternal," recurrence cannot be discussed without considering the question of *what* recurs or returns: the Same.

Taken in isolation, recurrence and return both involve at least two qualities: the quality of being unfinished and the quality of being interrupted. What has finished, what has reached its end, does not come again. What persists without interruption cannot come again, because it, so to speak, never gets away from itself.

The greatest difficulty with Nietzsche's word for the Same is that there is no exact equivalent for it in English. Nietzsche's expression *das Gleiche* is rather unusual in this context. He could just as well have said *ewige Wiederkehr des Selben*, and his thought would have been interpreted in the same manner as it has been, insofar as this has happened seriously at all.

Das Gleiche does *not* express simple identity, and therefore does not, strictly speaking, mean the Same. It lies somewhere between the Same and the Similar, but means neither exactly. For example: If two women have the same hat on, they have, strictly speaking, one hat on at different times. (One borrowed or stole the other's hat.) If two women have the "same" (in the sense of *gleich*) hat on at the same time, they have two hats which resemble each other so exactly that one could think that one woman had borrowed the other's hat, if one saw these women at different times. This is more than similarity, but it is not identity. Had Nietzsche meant "similar," his whole thought of recurrence would have been a commonplace triviality.

Etymologically, the German *gleich* is related to the English *like*, which meant originally "to have the same body."

The problem of the Same is the problem of "what" recurs. If the Same is not simply taken as the *content* stuffed into a prefabricated scheme of "eternal recurrence," a content totally indifferent to the process of recurrence, it becomes even more problematic and challenges the whole meaning of the phrase "eternal recurrence of the Same." If the Same were simply this indifferent, dead content caught up in recurring cycles, it would make no difference whether it was a thing or a tree or a man which recurred. The essential passages—that is, those in which Nietzsche is trying to think out the meaning of his thought, and not to "prove" it with the concepts of limited force and unlimited time (even these are very fruitful when not taken at a pseudoscientific level)— render an understanding of the Same as *content* impossible.

The alternative to understanding the Same as content is not to understand it as form, which would not make much sense in this context anyhow, but to think the Same *together with* Nietzsche's thought of eternal return as a whole. Admittedly, this is difficult, but it must be attempted. It requires one to think the Same as some sort of process, since there is no static content, no "what" or substance, in the traditional sense, in Nietzsche's thought. Nietzsche's thought concerns process, more exactly time and eternity, and it also concerns man in an eminent sense. Hence we have Nietzsche's emphasis on eternal return as a *thought*, even as a doctrine, and his tremendous concern about the effect of this thought on man.

If these considerations are put aside, man becomes one among all the other "same" things, same contents, and recurs in the deterministic fatalism of eternal recurrence. Eternal return has to do with fate, above all with *amor fati*,[2] but not with fatalism, an easy substitute for real thinking which Nietzsche would probably put on the level of Schopenhauer's pessimism.

The interpretation of eternal recurrence as the endless self-annihilating repetition of the same content is truly a nihilistic one. The nihilism of this interpretation lies not so much in calling the Same a content as in the unconditioned dominance of endless duration without a finale. This endless duration is *purely formal—* that is, it is totally indifferent to any event or the meaning of any event in it, and this indifference *determines* from the outset any possible "content," rendering it meaningless and irrelevant. Duration is that which is unable to end and is thus forced incessantly to demand another "content" to fill it out, preferably a content most nearly equal to the previous ones, in order to be able to present itself as something enduring, as substance. What cannot end must determine itself as an endlessly self-repeating content. Behind the "appearance" (the actual event) remains the essence (static duration established from the outset). The actual individual event can never exhaust the "Whole" (of already extended duration), can never be sufficient for it, can never even touch it or get at it, but remains indifferent to it. Thus the actual event must repeat itself again and again because something is *left over*.

If, however, time is not thought of as a perpetually remaining duration, as the framework *in which* recurrence recurs, then this

---

[2] As against Spinoza's *amor dei*.

meaning of the Same as the same content in "another," yet not "new," time becomes irrelevant. It becomes impossible to think of the Same as something "in time." If one tried to think the Same as temporal content in *this*—nondurational—time, its meaning would be that which time holds within itself, holds in an "In" which continually comes to pass again and again. This "In" is *not* the in of "in time," the static form in which something inexplicably "happens."

One passage from the *Nachlass* brings out this new conception particularly well: "If only *one* moment of the world came again, *all* would have to come again."[3] One can see here that it is time itself, the moment, which comes again, not something which is "in time."

Does not this, however, make time into a meaningless, atomistically discontinuous becoming, a concept which Nietzsche himself discussed and rejected in his earlier works as the self-consuming of time, Chronos who devours his own children? The implicit discontinuity in Nietzsche's new conception is not that of something atomistic, indivisibly isolated, but is rather a negative rejection of continuous duration. It is one thing to start out with the idea of finitude as the passing away of a relatively enduring entity in time, attributing the "work" of this finitude, its being brought about, to time itself. It is a completely different thing to take as one's starting point the character of time's happening as something nondurational. If time itself is thought nondurationally—that is, as a continual instantaneity (of moments), finitude does not mean that what is in time cannot be maintained, held on to. One arrives at an absolute lack of substratum, which excludes any idea of finitude as the passing away of something relatively durational.

This characteristic of time as an absolute lack of substratum points toward something "neutral" in the nature of time, a neutrality which makes possible different structures of experienced time, but which by no means determines or necessitates them. This character of neutrality would make Nietzsche's entirely different interpretations of eternal return more comprehensible. Above all, it would also explain his tremendous emphasis on man's

[3] *Nachlass*, XII: 370.

attitude and relationship to eternal return, an emphasis which is absolutely incompatible with any kind of deterministic idea of recurrence.

After a brief discussion of the relation of neutrality to Nietzsche's thought of eternal return, we shall go back to the different implications of that thought as Nietzsche saw them.

Neutrality should not be confused with relativity or with indifference. The factor of irreversibility, which incontestably belongs to time, renders such an interpretation impossible. Nietzsche does not think a great chaos of time, in which anything can happen, or inevitably recurring cycles, or a European form of Buddhism, duration with an "in vain." But neither is this neutrality a kind of δύναμις, a possibility either in the general sense of being able to become anything or in the Aristotelian sense of being related and actualized toward a specific reality. Nietzsche does not have an entelechy, a having-the-end-in-itself. There is no end. This is his basic insight.

Telos

Eternal return does have something to do with an "end," however, if only because it has to do with time. This relation becomes clearer if one considers the implications of Nietzsche's interpretations of eternal return. These interpretations can be grouped roughly into the following categories: (1) a fact belonging to physics, (2) an impossibility, and (3) a thought. Contradictory as they may seem at first glance, these three possibilities are interrelated and involve the traditional philosophical problems of the subject-object split prevalent since Descartes. With regard to Nietzsche's thought, the split could be formulated as follows: Either eternal return is an inevitable, unquestionable "fact" of nature, and man is thus helplessly caught up in cycles of Becoming (although, in contrast to other beings, he is capable of realizing that he is trapped in them [eternal recurrence as "objective fact"]); or, eternal return is something which in some sense depends on man. The fact of consciousness itself alters the character of recurrence; there is no recurrence *an sich* (eternal return as subjective task).

Considering Nietzsche's three interpretations, we must study those strains of his thought which seek to break out of the traditional problem rather than stuff them back into the old frame-work, a fairly easy procedure well encouraged by sheer habit.

In light of Nietzsche's rejection of the traditional concepts of metaphysics—substance, subject, God as *ground* of the world, any kind of Beyond or Behind the world—one is inclined to take his thought of eternal return to mean a world of endless Becoming in which a finite part is allotted to man. One might ask why Nietzsche did not simply "heroically" affirm this situation, as many thinkers before and after him have affirmed comparable situations.

This "situation," however, is nothing which Nietzsche sought to affirm. In fact, there was for him no such established situation. Eternal return as "vision and enigma" was what Nietzsche saw and what raised the tremendous question: Where, where do we belong?[4] The chapter in *Zarathustra* entitled "The Vision[5] and the Enigma" provides perhaps the most complete presentation of the thought of eternal return.

The tale begins when the ice of Zarathustra's heart breaks and he speaks:

To you, the daring venturers and adventurers, and whoever embarks with cunning sails on terrible seas—to you, the enigma-intoxicated, the enjoyers of twilight, whose souls are lured astray to every treacher-ous gulf, because you do not want to grope at a thread with cowardly hand; and where you can *divine*, there you hate to *calculate*—to you alone do I tell the enigma that I *saw*, the vision of the loneliest.[6]

Zarathustra then tells of his ascent upward in spite of the spirit drawing him downward, the spirit of gravity sitting on his shoulder in the form of a dwarf, paralyzed, paralyzing, dripping lead into his ear and thoughts like drops of lead into his brain.

The dwarf whispers in Zarathustra's ear: "You stone of wisdom! You threw yourself high, but every thrown stone must fall! . . . Far indeed have you thrown your stone—but it will fall back on yourself."[7] The dwarf then falls silent, and this silence finally be-

---

[4] *Nachlass* (Kröner ed.), vol. 83, p. 401.
[5] *Gesicht*, literally a "face," something *seen*.
[6] *Zarathustra*, III, "The Vision and the Enigma"; Thomas Common's translation, with some changes.
[7] *Ibid.*

comes so oppressive that Zarathustra's courage makes him stand still and say: "Dwarf! You!—or I!"

It is Zarathustra's courage which enables him to face the dwarf. Man is the most courageous animal. With his courage he has overcome every other animal.

Courage also slays dizziness at the edge of abysses: and where does man not stand at the edge of abysses? Is not seeing itself—seeing abysses?

Courage is the best slayer: courage slays even pity. But pity is the deepest abyss: as deeply as man sees into life, so deeply does he also see into suffering. Courage, however, is the best slayer, courage which attacks. It slays even death itself, for it says: "Was *that* life? Well! Once more!"[8]

Life, suffering, and the circle; these three belong inextricably together. When the vision Zarathustra describes in this chapter becomes reality later on, when he experiences what he has seen earlier, he calls himself the advocate of life, the advocate of suffering, the advocate of the circle. When he looks into life, he looks into suffering and into the "circle."

The situation with the dwarf is suddenly reversed by an act of courage. Zarathustra calls out: "Halt, dwarf! Either I—or you! I, however, am the stronger of us two—you do not know my abysmal thought. *That* you could not bear!"[9]

Instead of "you or I," Zarathustra can now say "I or you!" He has overcome the dwarf, who now springs from his shoulder. Zarathustra's thought is far more abysmal, goes deeper into life, suffering, and the circle than the spirit of gravity is able to do. Now that the spirit of gravity has been overcome, Zarathustra is free to communicate his abysmal thought. The two are at a gateway.

Behold this gateway, dwarf! It has two faces. Two roads come together here: no one has yet ever followed either to its end. This long lane backward continues for an eternity. And that long lane forward —that is another eternity. They contradict each other, these roads. They directly abut one another.[10] And it is here at this gateway that

[8] *Ibid.*
[9] *Ibid.*
[10] "Stossen sich gerade vor den Kopf."

they come together. The name of this gateway is inscribed above: "Moment." But whoever should follow one of them further—on and on, farther and farther—do you believe, dwarf, that these paths contradict each other eternally?[11]

The dwarf then murmurs contemptuously: "All that is straight lies, all truth is crooked, time itself is a circle."[12] At this Zarathustra becomes very angry and retorts: "You, spirit of gravity, do not make things too easy for yourself!"[13] He then continues:

Observe this moment! From this gateway, moment, a long, eternal lane runs *backward*: behind us lies an eternity. Must not whatever *can* run its course of all things have already run along that lane before? Must not whatever *can* happen have happened, have been done, have passed by before? And if everything has been there before—what do you think, dwarf, of this moment? Must not this gateway, too, have been there before? And are not all things knotted together so firmly that this moment draws after it *all* that is to come? *Therefore*—itself too? For whatever *can* run its course of all things—also into this long lane *outward*, too—it *must* run it once more! And this slow spider which crawls in the moonlight, and this moonlight itself, and I and you in the gateway, whispering together, whispering of eternal things —must not all of us have been there before? And return and run in that other lane before us, in that long, dreadful lane—must we not eternally return? Thus I spoke, more and more softly; for I was afraid of my own thoughts and the thoughts behind my thoughts.[14]

Here ends Zarathustra's communication of his abysmal thought. Following this passage he describes the overcoming of the abysmal in his thought—in other words, its transformation. But the thought as such is communicated completely in this passage, implicitly in all its possibilities. Everything in this passage belongs to the thought of eternal return as its *possibility*, but not to *the* possibility which Zarathustra is seeking and which he describes in the transformation that follows.

The image which Zarathustra gives is that of a gateway, the moment. This gateway has two faces, one toward the long lane continuing backward for an eternity (the past), the other toward

[11] *Zarathustra*, III, "The Vision and the Enigma."
[12] *Ibid.*
[13] *Ibid.*
[14] *Ibid.*

the long lane continuing "outward" for an eternity (the future). These two roads come *together* in the moment. They bump into each other. No one has ever gone to the end of these two roads. When they meet in the moment, they "contradict each other." What is the meaning of this?

First of all, it is important to note that Zarathustra does not say that the road of the future leads *forward,* as one would expect in correspondence to the road of the past leading *backward.* The road of the future leads "outward."[15] When Zarathustra speaks of the lanes leading away from the moment, he speaks primarily— really exclusively—of the lane backward. *Behind* us lies an eternity. What is *able* to run its course must already have happened. Only from this consideration of the eternity of the past does Zarathustra ask the dwarf: "Must not the moment, too, have already been there, must it not draw all things to come after it, itself included?" Zarathustra distinguishes between the lanes of the past and the future, and his question to the dwarf is oriented toward the eternity of the *past.*

Zarathustra then states that no one has ever gone to the end of these roads. This is important. Zarathustra asks the dwarf whether these roads would eternally contradict each other, should one follow one of them on and on. The implication is that somehow, "out there," past and future, each eternal (endless), will meet and form a circle, thus no longer contradicting each other. To this the dwarf mumbles contemptuously: "All that is straight lies, all truth is crooked, time itself is a circle." Hearing the dwarf's "wisdom," Zarathustra becomes angry and replies: "Do not make things too easy for yourself."

For Zarathustra, time is precisely *not* a circle. If no one has ever gone to the end of these roads, it is not possible for anyone to "come again," in the sense of having gone to the end of the eternal future to the point where it meets the eternal past, forming a circle and removing the mutual contradiction of past and future.

Last of all, Zarathustra states that these two roads contradict each other, not "out there" leading in opposite directions that

[15] *Hinaus.*

eventually meet, but in the *moment*, which has nothing to do with "leading" anywhere. Past and future come together in the *moment*, not out there (where?) in an eternal continuance directed *away from* the moment. It is the moment in which past and future meet with which Zarathustra is really concerned here, but the dwarf is unable to understand this. Thus he comes up with the quick and easy answer: "Time is a circle."

What does Nietzsche mean when he says that the roads *contradict* each other in the moment? The moment does not draw all *past* things after it into the future; it draws all *coming* things after it. This seems to mean that the moment draws all the future into the past, and it does this because all things are so *firmly* knotted together. If all things were not firmly knotted together, the future would not at all necessarily be drawn into the past. It is not so much the moment which draws everything as it is this firm connection of all things, a connection outside of the moment itself. Only when one *leaves* the moment itself (thus making it relinquish its character as moment) can the moment be fitted into the firm connection by which all things are drawn into the past.

Nietzsche's statement that in an eternal past all things must have already happened also implies a *determination* of the nature of all coming things. What is to come is precisely what has already been, since *all that is* lies in the eternal past. Past and future are basically "the same." Wherein lies the contradiction between them then? As soon as one *leaves* the moment, there is no contradiction of past and future, neither out there where they supposedly meet nor in their character as past and future, for what was in the past comes again as the future through the indifferent gateway of the moment.

It is important in this image to distinguish between what is "spatial," spatial in the broadest possible sense of extension, of what is there in a continuous manner, and what is "temporal." The two long, eternal lanes leading away from the moment are "spatial"; otherwise they could never meet to form a circle, nor could they be called roads or lanes. The moment itself, as an indifferent gateway through which past and future roll, also is spatial. It has nothing to do with the past or the future, or for that matter with the present; it simply lets the flux of time roll through it.

The meeting of past and the future in the moment is *not* spatial. "Roads" do not contradict each other. One can always go "farther," as long as there is a road. If Nietzsche had used the word "meet" in its usual sense, the temporal meaning of his thought would have been lost, and one road could have led into the other. But by saying that the past and the future contradict each other in the moment, he forces us to enter the moment itself, to stop, not to go on.

How can the past and the future possibly contradict each other? Certainly they do not when time is conceived of as continuously flowing time (in which the future flows into the past), or, as has also been maintained, when time is conceived of as a function of organic growth or as a historical process (whereby the past flows into the future). The fact that the *direction* of time, which is supposed to be irreversible, has these two mutually exclusive interpretations, is evidence of a real problem.

The flux of time, no matter what its "direction," cannot produce a contradiction. A "contradiction" can occur only in the moment.

There are two other passages in *Zarathustra* where "contradiction" is spoken of in a similar manner:

Where all becoming seemed to me the dance of gods and the prankishness of gods, and the world seemed free and frolicsome and fleeing back to itself—as an eternal fleeing and seeking each other again of many gods, as the blissful contradiction of each other, hearing of each other again, belonging to each other again of many gods.[16]

Where all time seemed to me a blissful mockery of moments, where necessity was freedom itself playing blissfully with the sting of freedom.[17]

The play on words here is somewhat difficult to render in English. The phrase *Sich-wider-sprechen* is transformed by the meaning of the following two phrases—to hear each other again, to belong to each other again—from its literal meaning of speaking *against* (*wider*) each other to that of speaking to each other *again* (*wieder*).

[16] "Das selige Sich-widersprechen, Sich-wieder-hören, Sich-wieder-zugehören vieler Götter." *Zarathustra*, III, "On Old and New Tables."
[17] *Ibid.*

When this speaking to each other again of many gods occurs, time becomes a blissful mockery of moments, of moments in the sense of a succession of disrupted, indifferent instants or "nows." Past and future meet in the moment, and nowhere else. Past and future, and thus all time, thus the eternal return itself, are *in the moment*. The ever-recurring phrase in the plans of the *Nachlass*—midday and eternity—shows that Nietzsche was preoccupied with this question.

The rest of the section entitled "The Vision and the Enigma" portrays the overcoming of the thought of eternal return in its abysmal character. The dwarf, no longer able to keep up with what is going on at all, disappears. Suddenly Zarathustra sees a shepherd lying on the ground, choking to death from a heavy black snake hanging out of his mouth. Horror and nausea are expressed in the convulsed face of the shepherd. He had gone to sleep, and the snake had crawled into his throat and bit itself fast there.

The snake is, of course, the abysmal thought of eternal recurrence, which crawled into the shepherd's throat while he was sleeping. Zarathustra tries to pull the snake out of the shepherd's throat, but in vain.

"Then it cried out of me—'Bite! Bite its head off! Bite!'"[18] The shepherd can save himself only by his own action, by biting off the *head* of the snake. No amount of pulling from outside can help him; it only aggravates his plight.

Zarathustra then asks: "*Who* is this shepherd into whose throat the snake crawled? *Who* is the man into whose throat all that is heaviest and blackest *will* crawl?"[19] This question is answered in a later chapter called "The Convalescent." What happens to the shepherd after he bites off the snake's head? He jumps up,

No longer shepherd, no longer a man, a transformed, radiant being who laughed. Never on earth has a human being laughed as he laughed. Oh my brothers, I heard a laughter that was no human laughter—And now a thirst gnaws at me, a longing that never grows still. My longing for this laughter gnaws at me. Oh, how do I bear to go on living? And how could I bear to die now![20]

[18] *Ibid.*, "The Vision and the Enigma."
[19] *Ibid.*
[20] *Ibid.*

41

This concludes the experience of the thought of eternal return as told in "The Vision and the Enigma." In the later chapter "The Convalescent," Zarathustra *undergoes* this same experience. What is most astonishing here is that the experience is totally new. No reference is made to the shepherd or to what happened to him. It is as if Zarathustra knew nothing about him at all. Even more astonishing is the fact that, having seen the shepherd's transformation, having seen the possibility of overcoming this abysmal thought and the intense joy which followed that act, Zarathustra can derive no help from the insight at all. One would think the experience would be familiar to him and the knowledge of its possible outcome a bulwark in the face of horror and disgust. But this is not the case. It is as if this experience, when actually lived and not just envisioned, were intrinsically unique and not to be anticipated, as if it would be new and unique however often it occurred. Evidently there is no cushioning through past experience here. The experience is starkly immediate.

Zarathustra's experience in "The Convalescent" begins as follows:

One morning, not long after his return to his cave, Zarathustra sprang up from his couch like a madman, crying with a frightful voice, and acting as if someone still lay on the couch who did not wish to rise. Zarathustra's voice also resounded in such a manner that his animals came to him frightened, and out of all the neighboring caves and lurking-places all the creatures slipped away—flying, fluttering, creeping, or leaping, according to their variety of foot or wing. Zarathustra, however, spake these words:

"Up, abysmal thought out of my depth! I am your cock and morning dawn, you overslept reptile: Up! Up! My voice shall soon crow you awake!

"Unbind the fetters of your ears: listen! For I wish to hear you!

"Up! Up! There is thunder enough to make the very graves listen!

"And rub the sleep and all the dimness and blindness out of your eyes!

"Hear me also with your eyes: my voice is a medicine even for those born blind.

"And once you are awake, then you shall ever remain awake. It is not *my* custom to awake great-grandmothers out of their sleep that I may bid them—sleep on!

"You stir, stretch yourself, wheeze? Up! Up! Not wheeze, shall you
—but speak to me! Zarathustra calls you, Zarathustra the godless! I,
Zarathustra, the advocate of life, the advocate of suffering, the advocate of the circle—you do I call, my most abysmal thought! Joy to
me! You come—I hear you! My abyss *speaks,* my lowest depth have I
turned over into the light!

"Joy to me! Come hither! Give me your hand—Ha! Let be! Aha!—
Disgust, disgust, disgust—alas to me!"[21]

The figure still lying on Zarathustra's bed is the figure of his
most abysmal thought, the thought which must emerge from *his*
depths. This thought is not some idea "outside" Zarathustra, it is
within him and can only be encountered as an inner truth. Zarathustra challenges his abysmal thought in a manner similar to that
in which he challenged the dwarf, but the challenge is far more
difficult this time. An abyss is less easily dealt with than a dwarf.
The commands with which Zarathustra calls out his thought are
peculiarly dialectical. The dialectical element lies in the relationship of listening and being heard and in the question: Who is
being awakened? In the beginning it is Zarathustra who commands
his thought to arise, to awaken with the words: "Listen! For I
wish to hear you!" The relationship between Zarathustra and his
abysmal thought is of such an intimate nature that no one-sided
speaking or listening is possible. Only when his thought listens can
it speak. The implication is that there is to be a real encounter between Zarathustra and his abysmal thought in which both must
listen and speak to each other and thus be transformed. It is also
important to note that Zarathustra says to his thought: "And
when you are once awake, you shall remain awake eternally for
me." Once this thought has emerged from the depths, it will
remain awake eternally. It seems strange that a thought, which is
normally an object of consciousness having no awareness or life of
its own, should take on the characteristics of a living being awakening from sleep. This strengthens the growing realization that
Zarathustra's abysmal thought is not a thought in the usual sense
of that word.

Whereas it is Zarathustra who is attempting to awaken his
thought, the actual effect is that he is overpowered by it and him-

[21] *Ibid.,* "The Convalescent."

self loses the state of wakefulness. The abysmal thought is so
powerful and of such an incalculable nature that Zarathustra falls
down as if dead and remains in this state for seven days. All his
preparations and foreknowledge are of no avail. He has succeeded
in bringing his last depths to light, but what he sees overwhelms
him.

With this the thought disappears, as did the dwarf, but for
opposite reasons. The dwarf disappeared because he could no
longer understand. The abysmal thought "disappears" because it
is no longer hidden in Zarathustra's depths. It has become an integral part of him during the seven days when he lay as if dead.

Again the dwarf does not interpret the meaning of what has
happened to Zarathustra; Zarathustra's animals do. The dwarf, the
spirit of gravity, made everything too *easy* for himself. The animals
do not do so. They are Zarathustra's animals, but they are animals.
The meaning they give to what has happened is, so to speak,
"true," but it is not "understood."

O my animals, answered Zarathustra, talk on thus and let me listen!
It refreshes me so to hear your talk: where there is talk, there is the
world as a garden to me.

How charming it is that there are words and tones; are not words and
tones rainbows and seeming bridges between the eternally separated?[22]

Zarathustra's animals are not "wrong," but the very fact that
they speak, that they *chatter* as Zarathustra says, builds illusory
bridges over that which is eternally separated. Words cannot even
touch upon the experience which Zarathustra has undergone.

The animals speak of being. The wheel of being rolls eternally,
the year of being runs eternally, the same house of being builds
itself eternally. The ring of being remains eternally true to itself.
Being begins in every moment.

It is as if the animals proclaim the truth of being in an extremely
opaque way. The meaning of what they say is not immediately
apparent. It preserves an enigmatic character.

When Zarathustra speaks to his animals, he explains that what
choked him was his disgust at mankind, above all at the small

22 *Ibid.*

44

man. But the fundamental statement of what he could not bear lies in the words: "Everything is alike, nothing is worthwhile, knowledge strangles." The thought of eternal return in its nihilistic form paralyzed Zarathustra. If everything is alike and recurs endlessly in meaningless monotony, life is not worth living, and the knowledge of this situation paralyzes man. For this reason Zarathustra's fate becomes that of the teacher of eternal return, for which he must find and communicate another meaning.

THREE INTERPRETATIONS

A Fact Belonging to Physics

In the Nachlass fragments we shall consider here, Nietzsche attempts to describe the nature of the cosmos with the help of the concepts of force, time, finitude, and infinity. These fragments are not the musings of a dilettante physicist. Nietzsche performed no experiments and calculated no conclusions. He is thinking out the presuppositions, the possibilities, and the implications of his thought. Here, too, his main concern is the basic problem "there is no end."

The two basic ideas which constitute these fragments are: force is finite; time is infinite.

The amount of total force is limited, nothing "infinite"; let us avoid such vagaries of the concept. Hence the number of states, changes, combinations, and developments of this force is tremendously large and practically "immeasurable," yet definite and not infinite. Time, however, in which the totality uses its force, is infinite—that is, force is eternally the same and eternally active. Up to this moment an infinity has passed—that is, all possible developments must have already been there. Consequently the development of this moment must be a repetition and thus that development which gave birth to it, and that which originates from it, and thus on and on forward and backward.[23]

[23] Nachlass, XII: 51. For a discussion of Nietzsche's "proofs" for eternal recurrence, see Oskar Becker, "Nietzsches Beweise für seine Lehre von der ewigen Wiederkunft," Gesammelte Philosophische Aufsätze (Pfullingen: Verlag Neske, 1963).

Nietzsche speaks here of force,[24] not power. He generally uses the word "force" when speaking of the cosmos without specific reference to man. The word "power" is more basic; it encompasses the totality of the "world" with particular reference to man. Power and force are not the same. Force might be called a primitive form of power applied to a restricted interpretation of nature. Power exists only in the form of increasing power over. The Will to Force would be a far less meaningful concept.

According to Nietzsche, force must be limited; otherwise it would disperse itself and be totally ineffectual. We speak of "gathering one's forces," by which we mean a collecting and concentration of resources. "The world, as force, cannot be conceived of as infinite. . . . We forbid ourselves the concept of *infinite force as being incompatible with the concept 'force.'*"[25]

The other idea in these fragments is that of infinite time, in which finite force works itself out. Rejecting any sort of creation or beginning of the world, Nietzsche shows that the supposedly self-contradictory concept of an infinity of past time stems from confusion.

Several attempts have been made lately to show that the concept that "the universe has an infinite past" (*regressus in infinitum*) is contradictory; it was even demonstrated, it is true, at the price of confounding the head with the tail. Nothing can prevent one from calculating backward from this moment of time and saying: "I shall never reach an end"; just as I can calculate forward from this same moment on out into infinity. It is only when I wish to commit the error—I shall be careful to avoid it—of equating this correct concept of a *regressus in infinitum* with the *absolutely unrealizable* concept of an infinite progress up to now, only when I take the *direction* (forward or backward) as logically indifferent, would I get the head—this moment—as the tail. . . .

If the universe were in any way able to congeal, dry up, die out, become *nothing*; or if it could attain a state of equilibrium; or if it had any kind of goal at all which included duration, immutability, a once-and-for-all (in short, to speak metaphysically, if becoming were able to resolve itself into being or into nothingness), this state ought already to have been reached. . . . This is the only certainty which we have

---

[24] *Kraft.*
[25] *The Will to Power*, 1062.

to serve as a corrective to a host of possible world hypotheses. If, for example, mechanism cannot escape the consequences of a final state, . . . then mechanism is thereby refuted.

If the world may be conceived of as a definite quantity of force and as a definite number of centers of force—and every other conception remains indefinite and therefore unusable—it follows from this that the world must go through a calculable number of combinations in the great dice-game of existence. In an infinite time every possible combination must have once been realized at some time; still more, it must have been reached an infinite number of times. And since between every one of these combinations and its next recurrence all other possible combinations must have elapsed and since every one of these combinations determines the whole sequence of combinations in the same order, a cycle of absolutely identical series is thus proven: the world as cycle which has already repeated itself an infinite number of times and which plays its game into infinity. This conception is not simply mechanistic; if it were, it would not bring about an infinite recurrence of identical cases, but a final state. Because the world has not reached a final state, mechanism is an imperfect and purely provisional hypothesis.[26]

The first part of this passage bears a curious resemblance to the dwarf's understanding of eternal recurrence. Nietzsche stresses the necessity of starting from the moment in the calculation of infinity. One cannot start back somewhere in infinity and calculate up to the present. This kind of beginning would be impossible, and, even if it could be done, one would arrive at the present moment —that is, at an end. Nietzsche starts from the present moment, but he leaves it to calculate backward and forward, thus substantiating his thesis that there is no end.

The second part of the passage is more important. It has to do with the impossibility of a once-and-for-all, a final state, not with the possibility of infinite calculation. The present state of "becoming" proves that no (static) being or nonbeing, no goal, no duration, no immutability, is possible. If any "end" were possible, it would have to have already been reached in the infinite past. Then, however, there would be no present state at all, let alone a present state of becoming, because, once attained, an end, a state of equilibrium, would persist. Nothing could ever disrupt it, get it started again.

[26] *Ibid.*, 1066.

It is interesting to note that Nietzsche rejects mechanism as a concept which cannot escape this final state. He often discusses mechanism, rejecting it on the grounds that, because it only describes quantities, it cannot explain the phenomenon of force: "The mechanistic concept wants nothing but quantities: but force lies in quality. Mechanism can thus only describe processes, not explain them." [27]

The rejection of mechanism and quantitative, "scientific" explanations leads to Nietzsche's concept of the Will to Power:

Could not all *quantities* be tokens of *qualities?* Another consciousness, another feeling, another desire, another way of looking at things corresponds to greater power; growth itself is a desire to *be more;* the desire for a More of quantum grows out of a quale; in a purely quantitative world everything would be dead, rigid, motionless—the reduction of qualities to quantities is nonsense. What happens is that one thing and another stand together, an analogy.[28]

Evidently Nietzsche feels that a mechanistic concept of force is inadequate, that mechanism is a dead and rigid explanation of the universe. A mechanistic universe would "run down" if it were ever even able to get started. The only aspect of mechanism which Nietzsche seems to accept is the constancy of the amount of energy present in the universe. But this quantitative factor only guarantees the limits of force, since Nietzsche considers the idea of unlimited force incompatible with the essence of force itself. The quantitative factor explains nothing about the nature of force. When Nietzsche attempts to explain the nature of force, he often uses the rather unusual word "economical."

Regarded mechanistically, the energy of the totality of becoming remains constant; regarded economically, it rises to a high point and sinks down again in an eternal circle. This "will to power" expresses itself in the interpretation, in the manner in which force is used up; transformation of energy into life, and "life at its highest potency," thus appears as the goal. The same quantum of energy means different things at different stages of evolution.

[27] *Ibid.*, 660.
[28] *Ibid.*, 564.

That which constitutes growth in life is an ever more thrifty and more far-seeing economy, which achieves more and more with less and less force. As an ideal, the principle of the smallest expenditure.

That the world is not striving toward a stable condition is the only thing that has been proved. Consequently one must conceive of its climatic condition in such a way that it is not a condition of equilibrium. The absolute necessity of similar events occurring in the course of one world, as in all others, is in eternity *not* a determinism which rules events, but merely the expression of the fact that the impossible is not possible; that a certain force cannot be any other than this certain force; that it can react to a quantum of resisting force only according to the measure of its strength; event and necessary event are a *tautology*.[29]

This fragment relates the concepts of eternal return and the Will to Power to each other. The difference between force and the Will to Power lies in the question of interpretation, of how force is used. The Will to Power does not strive to maintain itself; it strives for "life at its highest potency." A bare quantum of energy has no intrinsic meaning of its own. Meaning is present only at the level of the Will to Power. The Will to Power is neither an infinite striving nor does it strive for a state of equilibrium. If the Will to Power were infinite striving, this would contradict the nature of force and the ultimate result would be self-dispersion, not power. If the Will to Power strove for a state of equilibrium, it would strive for its own destruction in the form of a static state which could never be overcome. The climactic condition of the Will to Power is not equilibrium but rising to a high point. After the high point the Will to Power sinks down again in an eternal circle. Nietzsche does not specify here how one should conceive of this eternal circle, but it is this circle which guarantees the self-renewal of the Will to Power. Thus there is no contradiction between the constant striving for increase of the Will to Power and the eternal sameness of the eternal circle or eternal return. Each requires the other.

A final, highly enigmatic fragment might be cited here in connection with the "physics" of eternal return. "The two most ex-

[29] *Ibid.*, 639.

treme modes of thought—the mechanistic and the Platonic—are reconciled in the *eternal recurrence*: both as ideals."[30]

Mechanism as one extreme mode of thought would surely mean an explanation of the world in "objective" terms, of forces, efficient causality—in short, of the "billiard-ball" universe of the Enlightenment which needs nothing ideal or intellectual to explain it. Platonism, as the other extreme mode of thought, would mean an "ideal" interpretation of the universe in which the physical is at best the condition of what happens, but never the cause. The reality of Platonism lies in the Idea. It is questionable whether or not Nietzsche would understand the ideality of Platonism as something purely subjective. He often does in other contexts and, if he did here, he would have come up with a formulation of eternal recurrence in terms of the most extreme subject-object split. Eternal recurrence is either purely subjective or purely objective, mechanistic or Platonistic. According to Nietzsche, these two extremes are *reconciled* in eternal recurrence, both as ideals. What could this mean?

In a global reformulation these two extremes become the problem of free will and determinism. Mechanism entails an objective world of forces that absolutely determine one another. There is no room for the possibility of anything happening differently from the way in which it was conditioned by its previous state. Or, in Nietzsche's words, event and necessary event are repetitious.

Platonism entails the possibility of man's shaping his life through inquiry and gaining insight into the realm of Ideas. Man can never attain this realm completely, but he strives for wisdom and can attain it at least in part. Applied to eternal return, this would mean that man is determined by objective forces causing him to recur along with all other beings, or he is free to gain insight into recurrence itself and thus to acquire control over his own fate.

A possible clarification of the reconciliation of these two extremes in eternal recurrence lies in the direction of a renewed consideration of Nietzsche's statement that there is no end. This statement admits of two interpretations, both of which Nietzsche

[30] *Ibid.*, 1061.

considered but never expressly related to each other. "There is no end" can mean, on the one hand, that the universe is endless and continues to recur endlessly in cycles. On the other hand, "there is no end" can also mean that nothing is ever completed at any given moment. Stripped of the framework implicit in the first interpretation of absolute Newtonian time, "recurrence" becomes something going on in every moment. The question in this case is not that of free will or determinism, but that of giving structure to possibilities that recur anew constantly. Man is free, but he is not free in the sense of complete, random arbitrariness or of fantastic omnipotence. Given the basis of the past he has accumulated by the time he becomes truly aware of himself, he can shape himself and his world in accordance with the possibilities open to him. Thus the discussion turns to two other possible interpretations of eternal return: (1) an impossibility and (2) a thought.

An Impossibility

Nietzsche's questions and doubts about eternal recurrence, many of which can be found in a passage from the *Nachlass* entitled "What I Have as a Counterhypothesis against the Cyclical Process," are intimately connected with his polemic against mechanism. These questions show that Nietzsche felt keenly the problems involved in his thought of recurrence, above all the problem of recurrence in a nonmechanistic (that is, non-"deterministic") world.

Is not the existence of *any* difference and incomplete circularity in the world around us already a *sufficient* disproof of a uniform circle of everything that exists? Where does the difference within the circle come from? Where does the temporal duration of this occurring difference come from? . . . Is it possible that different things can originate from "force"? Arbitrary things? Does the lawfulness which we see deceive us? Not be a primal law?[31]

Nietzsche raises several objections here: (1) Any differences or aberrations from perfect circularity question the pervasiveness and scope of that circularity. How is it possible for such differences to

[31] *Nachlass*, XII: 58–59.

originate within the supposedly already established circle, and what determines the extent of their existence and duration? From what source do they receive the power to exist if there is nothing apart from circularity? (2) How do we know that equal forces produce equal *things*? (3) How do we know that the laws of the circle which we observe are not temporary laws? How can we say that they are eternal?

Everything has already been there a countless number of times, insofar as the total state of all forces recurs again and again. Whether, *apart from this*, anything identical [*gleich*] has been there, is totally incapable of proof. It seems as if the total state forms *qualities* anew down to the smallest thing, so that two different total states cannot have anything identical [*gleich*].[32]

If it is only the general state of forces which "recurs" and if these forces form completely new qualities, the meaning of eternal recurrence becomes so vague that it simply evaporates. In this fragment Nietzsche is repudiating any sort of identity on the basis of the forces that build new qualities.

In another fragment he brings in the far more important question of an interpretation and understanding of these forces.

The exact same course, but a higher interpretation of that course! The mechanistic sameness of force, but an increase in the feeling of power! "The second time"—but there is no "second time." The absolute *lack of effect* of the inner feeling of power as causality.[33]

Nietzsche is speaking here about power. This is one of the few passages in which he explicitly relates his concept of force to his concept of power. Power is for Nietzsche more comprehensive than force. Power includes the full phenomenon of growth and increase, in both the natural and the human sphere. In this fragment the mechanistic sameness of force gives way before the increase of the feeling of power. The same process with a higher interpretation ceases to be the same process. There is no "second time," because essentially nothing repeats itself. If force cannot be isolated as a calculable factor—that is, if the "interpretation" and

[32] *Ibid.*, 51.
[33] *Ibid.*, XIII: 62.

meaning of force belong intrinsically to force itself and are not just external, arbitrary, subjective explanations for something which has already occurred, then this fragment must be understood as Nietzsche's serious objection to any mechanistic kind of recurrence. The end of the fragment is puzzling: "The absolute lack of effect of the inner feeling of power as causality." Power as a new kind of causality is consistent with what was said in the rest of the fragment. But what of the absolute lack of effect *as causality*? The contrast between mechanistically efficient causality and the "causality" of power could not be expressed more strongly. Nietzsche points here to a kind of causality which does not string itself out in a series of effects, but which rather remains within itself, remains absolutely without (this kind of) ef-fect.

The fragments that speak against the possibility of eternal recurrence as mechanistic recurrence point toward very enigmatic possibilities of "recurrence" in man himself. These possibilities require a total rethinking of the structure of human consciousness, of man in general.

The Will to Suffering: you creating ones, you must sometimes live in the world. You must *almost* be destroyed—and afterward *bless* your labyrinth and your confusion. Otherwise you could not *create*, but only die *off*. You must have your rise and decline. You must have your bad traits and sometimes take them upon yourselves again. You eternally returning ones, you yourselves should make a recurrence out of yourselves.[34]

The alternatives of creating or dying off remind one of Nietzsche's remarks about life and the Will to Power. Nothing can remain stable. If a living thing does not increase, it must decrease. There is no such thing as the Will to Live. What is alive does not need to strive for life. What is not alive cannot strive at all.

In order to create, man must be willing to face near destruction, to let go of everything he has. Only by doing this is it possible for something *new* to come into being, for something to be created. Without destruction or near destruction there can be no creation.

[34] *Ibid.*, XII: 251.

In *Zarathustra*, Nietzsche had said that three things belong indissolubly together: life, suffering, and the circle. The connection between life and suffering is perhaps the easiest to understand. Life inextricably involves the pain of loss, the pain of rebirth after emerging from hard experiences. It is the more abstract term "circle" which seems curious in its connection with life and suffering. Nietzsche obviously does not mean the circle of geometry, but rather a structure of life. If the mechanistic interpretation of eternal recurrence is an impossibility, the idea of the circle points toward a structure of recurrence or return which is not mechanistic and not naturalistically determined.

There are two main strains of emphasis on eternal return which seem at first to be contradictory. On the one hand, Nietzsche emphasizes the inevitable, fate-full character of recurrence. There is no getting away from it. It is the inexorable law of the world. On the other hand, Nietzsche calls upon man to use his creative power in the shaping of his own fate. It is to this latter emphasis that Nietzsche's questions about the impossibility of eternal recurrence belong. The arguments against eternal recurrence seem to be less concerned with stating that something cannot be so than with stating that it *must* not be so. To counteract the looming possibility of eternal recurrence in its nihilistic form, a transformation is necessary.

To *endure* the idea of recurrence one needs: freedom from morality; new means against the fact of *pain* (pain conceived of as a tool, as the father of pleasure; there is no *cumulative* consciousness of displeasure); the enjoyment of all kinds of uncertainty, experimentalism, as a counterweight to this extreme fatalism; abolition of the concept of necessity; abolition of the "will"; abolition of "knowledge in itself."

Greatest elevation of the consciousness of strength in man, as he who creates the superman.[35]

This transformation, achieved through the intensification of uncertainty, temptation, through the removal of the concepts of necessity, will, and knowledge in itself, aims at the highest possible elevation of the consciousness of force (power) in man. If

[35] *The Will to Power*, 1060.

ideas such as necessity, will, and knowledge in itself, which reign above man and crush his creative power, can be removed, the nihilistic form of eternal recurrence can also be removed.[36] This heaviest of all thoughts can be prevented through a transvaluation of all values.

1. The idea (of eternal recurrence): the presuppositions that would have to be true if it were true. Its consequences.
2. As the *hardest* idea: its probable effect if it were not prevented—that is, if all values were not transvalued.
3. Means of *enduring* it: the transvaluation of all values. No longer joy in certainty but in uncertainty; no longer "cause and effect" but the continually creative; no longer the will to preservation but to power; no longer the humble expression, "everything is subjective," but "it is also *our* work!—Let us be proud of it!"[37]

The emphasis shifts here from stating that perhaps eternal recurrence is impossible to questioning the possibility of overcoming eternal recurrence through the thought—that is, through the awakening consciousness—of eternal recurrence.

From the moment when this thought is there, all color changes and there is another *history*.

The most powerful thought uses up a great deal of force which previously served other aims; thus it has a *transforming* effect. It creates new laws of motion of force, but not new force. Herein lies the possibility of determining and ordering individuals in their dispositions in a new way.[38]

Seen in this light, the thought of eternal recurrence, particularly in its nihilistic, mechanistic form, becomes the highest obstacle to life. If this obstacle can be overcome, life will be elevated to a higher stage of self-surpassing, and the opposition between the Will to Power and eternal recurrence will vanish. "Life itself created this thought most difficult for life; it wants to overcome its highest obstacle."[39]

[36] See *ibid.*, 1057, where Nietzsche speaks of the means to remove eternal recurrence.
[37] *Ibid.*, 1059.
[38] *Nachlass*, XII: 65.
[39] *Ibid.*, 369.

A Thought

The majority of Nietzsche's statements about eternal recurrence are concerned with it as a *thought*. Eternal recurrence gains its true stature as a thought, not because it represents a kind of "as-if" philosophy, but because it brings in the decisive—that is, the decision-making—characteristic of man. Paradoxically stated, it is precisely the inevitability inherent in this thought which forces man to make a free decision. The freedom of the decision comes only as the fruit of a terrible struggle, and it culminates in Nietzsche's idea of *amor fati*, or the identity of the highest fatalism with the Creative.[40]

No matter what interpretation is given to eternal recurrence, it always remains a *thought*, for Nietzsche thought it, and whoever reads him is also presumably thinking about it. Even the "factual" emphasis of the first interpretation is basically just another way of *thinking* eternal recurrence. This is not to say that it is something "subjective." There is nothing arbitrary or subjective about Nietzsche's thought. The whole basis for such arbitrariness is lacking in his philosophy. On the other hand, his thought is not subject to a kind of "determinism," a complete subjection of the human being to some inscrutable mechanism of fate. Nietzsche's concern lies not in the subjection of man to fate but in man's relation to that fate. It makes no sense for man to prostrate himself on the ground before fate, because he himself belongs to, *is*, that fate. To prostrate oneself before oneself is comic.

Two passages, one from *The Wanderer and His Shadow* and one from *The Joyful Wisdom*, indicate that Nietzsche saw this problem of man and fate and rejected the usual position of determinism as an inability to think the problem out.

The whole attitude of "man *versus* the world," man as world-denying principle, man as the standard of the value of things, as judge of the world, who in the end puts existence itself on his scales and finds it too light—the monstrous impertinence of this attitude has dawned upon us as such, and has disgusted us; we now laugh when we find "Man *and* World" placed beside one another, separated by the sublime presumption of the little word "and"![41]

[40] *Ibid.*, XIV: 301.
[41] *The Joyful Wisdom*, 346.

Turkish fatalism. Turkish fatalism contains the fundamental error of placing man and fate opposite each other like two separate things: Man, it says, can strive against fate, can try to defeat it, but in the end it always remains the winner, for which reason the smartest thing to do is to give up or live just any way at all. The truth is that every man himself is a piece of fate; when he thinks he is striving against fate in the way described, fate is being realized here, too; the struggle is imaginary, but so is resignation to fate; all these imaginary ideas are included in fate. The fear which most people have of the doctrine of determinism of the will is precisely the fear of this Turkish fatalism. They think man will give up weakly and stand before the future with folded hands because he cannot change anything about it; or else he will give free rein to his total caprice because even this cannot make what is once determined still worse. The follies of man are just as much a part of fate as his cleverness: this fear of the belief in fate is also fate. You yourself, poor frightened man, are the invincible Moira reigning far above the gods; for everything which comes, you are blessing or curse and in any case the bonds in which the strongest man lies. In you the whole future of the human world is predetermined; it will not help you if you are terrified of yourself.[42]

The first quotation belongs to Nietzsche's critique of what he calls "wishfulness," wishfulness which decides that there must be such a thing as substance, subject, self, and so on. In this case it is the separation of man and world which is brought about, partly a separation in the form of man denying or judging the world; but beyond that it is the separation itself of which denying and judging are but remote consequences. The sublime presumption of this small word "and" leads us to think that man *and* world are two separable things.

In the second passage Nietzsche uses *fate* instead of *world*, but his meaning is basically the same as it was in the first passage. Fate is a more basic concept in Nietzsche's thought, for he does not reflect specifically on the possible meanings of *world* (such as "cosmos" or "*mundus*"). When Nietzsche reflects on the "world," he treats it mostly as "fate." This can be seen in the end of the last fragment (second version) of the *Will to Power*, where Nietzsche concludes:

[42] *The Wanderer and His Shadow*, 61; author's translation.

This world is the Will to Power—and nothing else! and you your-selves are this Will to Power—and nothing else![43]

"Nothing else" gives to this world the character of "fate," in the sense that there is nothing beyond, above, or behind it.

Turkish fatalism separates man and fate, or man and the world. In opposition to this, Nietzsche states that man himself is a piece of fate, or, more radically, that man himself is the invincible Moira. These two passages alone, if read carefully, are enough to show the impossibility of interpreting eternal recurrence either as an inevitable fact of nature (world, fate) or as a subjective arbitrari-ness on the part of man, who, belonging to fate itself, cannot suddenly disengage himself from the world and decide to do "any-thing he wants" (wishfulness).

In trying to think out the unity of man and fate (world), Nietz-sche himself was forced to move between these two incompatible forces. His moving back and forth is reflected also in his treatment of eternal recurrence. Nietzsche cannot suddenly jump out of the whole tradition and begin talking about the unity of man and fate with complete originality. Considering even the usual concept of "man" (rational animal), this would make no sense. Nietzsche is groping for a new concept of man seen in his unity with fate and eternal recurrence, for man is "the still undetermined animal."[44]

If fate is not to be equated with Turkish fatalism, it is nothing above man against which man is powerless (and thus exempt from really doing anything). Fate is *in* man. This is what is difficult to understand without lapsing into one or the other side of the old dichotomy.

Fatum is an elevating thought for him who comprehends that he belongs *to it*.[45]

The unconditioned necessity of all occurrence has no compulsion about it: he stands high in knowledge who has thoroughly realized and felt this.[46]

[43] *The Will to Power*, 1067.
[44] "Das noch nicht festgestellte Tier." See *Beyond Good and Evil*, in *The Philosophy of Nietzsche* (New York: Random House, Modern Library, 1954), p. 448.
[45] *Nachlass*, XIV: 99.
[46] *Ibid.*, XIII: 63.

58

Where there is no compulsion, there is no *external* force. Yet this is no everyday, automatic state of affairs; it is something to be felt and realized in a higher state of knowledge.

When Nietzsche expressly relates the idea of fate to the thought of eternal recurrence, his statements become more radical: "Highest fatalism, but identical with chance and the Creative. (No repetition in things, this must first be created.)"[47]

How is a repetition in things to be *created*? This seems highly enigmatic. It is in fact incomprehensible, as long as man and world are presumptuously separated by the little word "and." The fact that Nietzsche first crossed out the words in parentheses (no repetition in things, this must first be created), indicates that he was acutely aware of the boldness of his statement, but it does not mean that he rejected it. The same idea can be found in other passages: "You who eternally recur, you should yourselves make a recurrence out of yourselves."[48] Here it is not a recurrence in *things* which is to be created but a "recurrence" in man himself.

The final statement to be mentioned in this connection reads: "I myself am fate and have conditioned existence for all eternity."[49] This sounds either like mystification or delusions of grandeur, or both. But the "I" which Nietzsche is talking about here is not the individual ego of Friedrich Nietzsche. Neither is it the general "Self," which Nietzsche would reject as a fabrication of wishfulness. This "I" can be understood only on the basis of eternal return, which brings us now to the problem of the Self.

[47] *Ibid.*, XIV: 252.
[48] *Ibid.*, 307.
[49] *Ibid.*, XII: 252.

III

THE SAME

The "I," or the Self, which, until Hume, was conceived of as a kind of soul, substance, or subject—something remaining through change, experiencing that change, and in some sense forming a center of experience—is presumably expressed in the word "Same" in the phrase "eternal return of the Same."

What makes Nietzsche's thought of eternal return so difficult to approach is his attempt to think the "Same," the Self or consciousness, as something other than a behavioristically determined string of events, and as something other than the idealistically structured subject of reflection. If we do not probe into his attempt to think the Same, however, his thought of eternal return will remain either fantastic or trivial. The Same eternally returns. If there is no return, there is no Same. If this return is not in some (new) sense eternal, again there is no Same, only a temporary coincidence in the double meaning of that word: (1) chance and (2) a falling-together which does not constitute anything.

If the Self is a behavioristically determined string of events, then this "same" string recurs at fantastic intervals within the framework of Newton's absolute time (and space) without the slightest knowledge of recurrence or the slightest power to do anything about it. This form of the thought of recurrence obliterates any possible meaning of return, for a return in the strict sense requires some sort of consciousness which a string of events is *eo ipso* unable to produce.

On the other hand, there is nothing in Nietzsche's thought that corresponds to the return of the Absolute Spirit to itself (Hegel). Return cannot be equated with the reflection of the absolute subject. Hegel's absolute reflection constitutes its own time (as contrasted with events that wander about in an external framework of absolute time like a thing within another thing), but its time is completely determined by the structure of reflection itself, that is, by dialectic. In German Idealism the structure of dialectic is in itself, for itself, and in and for itself (Hegel), or a thesis, antithesis, and synthesis (Fichte). It is precisely this activity, this *positing*, which is lacking in Nietzsche's concept of the Self, or Same.

From the consideration of eternal return as a *thought*, we have arrived at the problem of consciousness and the Self, what Nietzsche calls the "Same." Eternal return as a *thought* is a possibility of being which involves a relation of the "Self" to time. It is not a *concept* within the framework of rationalism. Concepts are timeless. This does not mean that Nietzsche is "irrational," however. An irrational thinker is a contradiction in terms. An irrational thinker would have great difficulty writing anything, and, even if he succeeded in doing so, who would care to read it? *Thought* does not have to be equated entirely with conceptual logic. An artist who cannot "think" cannot produce a work of art. Yet, an artist who does produce one, will not by any means be primarily using conceptual logic. "Consciousness" cannot be reduced to logic or swallowed up by it. Yet this does not reduce all other kinds of consciousness to the level of "irrationalism." The "irrational" is the windmill opponent of rationalism. It is like Don Quixote's fight, which never gets off the ground. The bass note remains the same throughout all the *Sturm und Drang*. An irrational person is simply someone who is unable to think.

Nietzsche thinks the Self as the "Same" on the basis of eternal return. He thinks the Self together with time. He does not think the Self as substance.

This brings us to the brink of the real abyss, the problem of the Self. Nietzsche would say: "Is not seeing itself seeing abysses?"[1] Then he would say: "With eagle's talons grasp the abyss!"[2]

To sharpen our talons, the best grindstone might be the rough road from Descartes to Hegel, on which the smoothness of Descartes' *ergo* (*cogito ergo sum*) is ploughed up and dispersed by Hume, transcendentally salvaged by Kant (the Self or the "I think" is an a priori condition of all knowledge, but no *ergo* is permissible), and then is made a royal, world-historical throughway for the Absolute Spirit by Hegel. With Kant and Hegel, the Self enters into a relationship with time.

For Descartes the self is a finite (created) substance, a thinking thing. "I think, therefore I am; and what I am is a thinking thing."

When we perceive any attribute, we therefore conclude that some existing thing or substance to which it may be attributed is necessarily present.[3]

Because there is no substance which does not cease to exist when it ceases to endure, duration is only distinct from substance by thought.[4]

The indubitable attribute of thinking leads Descartes to the thinking thing, a substance characterized by duration.

To the famous dictum "*cogito ergo sum*" Nietzsche remarks: "He ought to have said: '*ergo est*' . . . instead of saying 'there is something, there exists something, something is'; one could just as well say 'something is going on there.'"[5]

Locke "localizes" the reality of Descartes' *res extensa* in primary qualities. Berkeley undercuts the distinction between primary and secondary qualities and places all reality in spirit (*esse est percipi*), ultimately in the Spirit, or God. Thus the whole burden of reality comes to rest on the somewhat precarious "Self."

Faithful to the method of empiricism, Hume asks about the idea of Self: "From what impression could this idea be derived?"[6] (No

[1] *Zarathustra*, III, "The Vision and the Enigma."
[2] *Ibid.*, IV, "The Higher Man."
[3] Descartes, *The Principles of Philosophy*, LII, in *Descartes: Selections*, ed. Ralph M. Eaton (New York: Scribners, 1955).
[4] *Ibid.*, LXII.
[5] *Nachlass*, XIV: 4.
[6] Hume, *Treatise on Human Nature*, sec. 6, "On Personal Identity," in *Hume on Human Nature* . . . (New York: Macmillan, Collier Classics, 1962).

impression, no idea.) "I never can catch *myself* at any time without a perception, and never can observe anything but the perception."[7] The "Self" is a bundle of impressions.

It was Kant's insight that the Self cannot be that to which our impressions and ideas have a reference. Impressions and ideas, or experience, are not *referred to* the Self; the Self is what makes experience *possible* as the synthesizing activity of its elements. Otherwise experience could never be *my* experience. The Self is neither phenomenon nor thing-in-itself, but rather the transcendental unity of consciousness which must be able to accompany all thinking. The Self is not a thing or a substance at all; it is what makes the unity of experience possible, what makes "experience" *my* experience.

Nothing is more natural or more seductive than the illusion of believing the unity in the synthesis of thinking to be a perceived unity in the subject of these thoughts. One could call this illusion the subreption of hypostasized consciousness (*apperceptionis substantiatae*).[8]

Kant's insight into the nature of the Self as a transcendental activity of synthesis brought the Self into an intimate, if somewhat inscrutable, relation to time. On all levels of transcendental synthesis it is time which makes the activity of the Self possible. The most basic level is that of the synthesis of sensations into intuitions, where time is the form of inner (and thus indirectly of all) sensibility. At the level of the imagination we find the schemata, which are a priori determinations of time according to rules (*Zeitreihe, Zeitinhalt, Zeitordnung, Zeitinbegriff*). In the imagination lies the common root of sensibility and concepts, a common root which Kant saw but could not fully think through. Finally, the Self is legitimately the "I think" which must be able to accompany all experience; it is "a feeling of existence."[9] Illegitimately, it becomes one of the ideas of pure reason, the soul. The "I think" is indeed the transcendental vehicle of all concepts, for it serves to introduce

[7] *Ibid.*

[8] Kant, *Gesammelte Schriften* (Berlin: Walter de Gruyter & Co., 1968), I: 766; author's translation.

[9] Kant, *Prolegomena*, trans. Paul Carus and Lewis W. Beck, rev. ed. (New York: Bobbs-Merrill, Library of Liberal Arts, 1950), no. 46.

all thought as belonging to consciousness. The step from the bare consciousness which accompanies all concepts to the transcendental subject of all thought—a subject characterized in the paralogisms as substance, as simple, as unity, and as related to possible objects in space—is a necessary, but unverifiable dialectical inference. The Self or consciousness is "not a representation distinguishing a particular object, but a form of representation in general." [10] On this level of synthesis, too, the intimate relation of the Self to time is preserved. They are both *forms of*. The Self is: (1) "transcendental consciousness of my existence in general"; (2) consciousness "of my existence in time" (empirical consciousness of myself); and (3) "knowledge of myself as a being determined in time" (empirical knowledge). [11]

With Hegel the relation of the Self to time becomes a real problem, a problem which Hegel glosses over transcendentally with characteristic sovereignty. The Self for Hegel is *not* substance. This is the gist of his whole polemic against Spinoza. The Self is a positing subject, ultimately the Absolute Spirit. This brings the Self into a genuine relationship to time, for it is essentially an activity. The nature and structure of this activity are dialectical, however; activity is a positing. It is precisely the relation of the predetermined structure of dialectic to the structure of time which Hegel cannot explain. Hegel's awareness of this difficulty is evident in his constant polemic against bad infinity (How are you going to *stop* time? When is the dialectical process *completed*? What prevents it from starting all over again?) and in his attempt to relegate time to an inferior sphere, to a mere externality yet to be elevated through dialectic into the higher sphere of the concept and thus overcome in its independent character by being incorporated into the concept.

For Hegel, time is "the same principle as the ego, the ego of pure self-consciousness," [12] but it is this principle only in its total externality and abstraction (*abstraction* in Hegel's characteristic use of the word as not yet concrete, as bare abstraction). At best,

[10] Kant, *Critique of Pure Reason*, trans. F. Max Müller (New York: Anchor Books, 1966), A347, B405.

[11] *Nachlass*, N6313.

[12] Hegel, *Encyclopedia*, no. 258; author's translation.

time belongs to the sphere of representation (*Vorstellung*); it does not reach the level of the concept (*Begriff*). "Time is the concept itself which is *there* and represents itself to consciousness as empty intuition."[13] It *confronts* consciousness as something foreign. For this reason the Spirit appears in time as long as it has not grasped its pure concept—that is, as long as it has not annihilated time as something outside itself.

Hegel thinks the Self, or Spirit, as activity, but he determines the structure of this activity in such a way that it is incommensurable with time. Hegel recognized this problem to some extent, and polemicized against it in his treatment of what he called "bad infinity," yet it remained a problem which he was never really able to cope with in a conclusive way.

It is in accordance with the concept of Spirit that the development of history should fall into time. Time contains the determination of the negative. Something is there, an event, positive for us; but that its opposite counterpart is contained within it, this relation to Non-being is time, in such a way that we don't just think this relation, but also intuit it. Time is this totally abstract Sensuousness. . . .

In nature things fall apart, and all individual buds remain existing beside each other; the transition appears only to the thinking spirit which grasps the connection. Nature doesn't grasp itself, and thus the negative of her forms is not present for her. In the spiritual realm, however, it becomes apparent that the higher form is produced through transformation of the earlier, lower form. The latter has thus ceased to exist; and that this becomes apparent, namely that one form is the transfiguration of the earlier form, this is the reason why the appearance of spiritual form falls into time. World history is thus in general the interpretation of Spirit in time, as is nature the interpretation of the idea in space.[14]

For Hegel, nature exists within the realm of the spatial. It never gets beyond the uniform repetition of the same kind of existence. Change is repetition of the same. A tree produces another tree of

---

[13] Hegel, *Phenomenology of Mind*, trans. J. B. Baillie (New York: Harper & Row, Torchbooks, 1967), sec. VIII, "Absolute Knowledge."

[14] Hegel, *Reason in History*, trans. Robert S. Hartman (New York: Bobbs-Merrill, Library of Liberal Arts, 1953), C, "The Course of World History," (a), "The Principle of Development."

its kind, not a higher form of a tree. There is no progress in nature as such.

In the realm of Spirit, however, change is for Hegel *eo ipso* progress. It is Hegel's claim that nothing new is produced in space, but that every development in time produces not only something new but something higher incorporating and containing the earlier stage. The development of Absolute Spirit is neither the uniform repetition of the Same, nor a progression into (bad) infinity. It is a development which returns to itself.

The concept of Spirit is return to itself, to make itself an object. Thus its progression is not an indeterminate one into infinity; rather is there an aim, namely the return to itself. Thus there is a certain cycle, spirit seeks itself.[15]

The structure of dialectic overcomes the repetition of nature and it also avoids endless progression, the not-being-able-to-stop of bad infinity. How is the structure of dialectic constituted so as to be able to do this, and how does its structure fit in with that of time, which in contrast to space affords the possibility of new development? Or does time itself have no structure? Is it simply a function or a by-product of the activity of dialectic? The latter would be the easiest answer for Hegel to give, an answer which would characterize time in such a manner that it could not interfere with the activity of dialectic. Hegel says, however, that the development of history *falls into* time. If time were nothing but a function or a by-product of the Spirit, the statement that the development of Spirit falls into time would present serious problems.

Hegel's dialectic is the dialectic of the Absolute Spirit. Its activity is essentially that of *positing*, of positing a thesis, an antithesis, and finally the synthesis of these two, which in turn becomes a new thesis for the further activity of the dialectic.

The development of Absolute Spirit falls into time because it must *unfold* dialectically. Hegel makes contradictions *move*; in fact, it is this very contradiction, or negativity, which makes the movement and unfolding of the Absolute Spirit possible. Hegel's claim is that the dialectical movement of Absolute Spirit *loses*

[15] *Ibid.*

67

nothing, but rather incorporates all that has gone before in a higher and more developed manner.

For Kant, time is a form of *intuition*, the form of inner sensibility; indirectly it is also the form of outer sensibility and ultimately of all possible experience. Time is thus essentially related to receptivity. For Hegel, time must be related to the *concept*. This means that time is essentially related (1) not to receptivity but to spontaneity, (2) to the universal (concept), and (3) to the activity of positing. Hegel tries to cope with the relation of time to the activity of positing in his philosophy of nature. His problem here is to relate positing, which is strictly a structure of conceptual consciousness, to time in nature.

Hegel states that the Spirit is commensurate with time because both have the structure of negation of negation. In the case of the Spirit, this is obvious. The negation of negation is synthesis as the negation of antithesis, which in turn is the negation of thesis. In the case of time, negation of negation is what Hegel calls punctuality—that is, not the *being* outside itself[16] of space, but a *coming* outside itself.[17]

Time is "intuited becoming."[18] When the point (of space) posits itself for itself, the *now* arises. Thus time is the concept which is *there*, and, "since Space is simply the inner negation of itself, thus the self-negating[19] of its moments is its truth; time is just the existence of this continual self-negation."[20]

Time is the activity, the actual taking place of continual self-negation. It is thus the truth of space. By *truth* Hegel means not some kind of correspondence between ideas and things, but the actual fact of existence, the being there of self-negation.

Time is the pure form of sensibility or intuition, the non-sensible Sensible. Time is the same principle as the $I = I$ of pure consciousness, but the same or the simple concept still in its total externality and abstraction as intuited mere becoming. . . . Pure Being-within-itself as an absolute Coming-outside-itself.[21]

[16] *Aussersichsein.*
[17] *Aussersichkommen.*
[18] *Das angeschaute Werden.*
[19] *Sichaufheben.*
[20] Hegel, *Encyclopedia*, sec. 257, "Zusatz"; author's translation.
[21] *Ibid.*, sec. 258; author's translation.

It is not in time that everything comes to be and passes away. Rather it is time itself which is this becoming, coming to be and passing away, the existing abstracting; Chronos who gives birth to all things and destroys them.[22]

Time is not a kind of container in which everything is placed as in a flowing stream which sweeps it away and destroys it. Time is only the abstraction of this consuming.[23]

Hegel's insight into the nature of time removes time from its traditional representation as some kind of container in which events flow or take place. Instead of inquiring further into the nature of time as an activity, as a kind of "self-occurrence," however, Hegel relegates it to the domain of externality. Time is mere Becoming; it is unrelated to the concept or to consciousness. Implicitly it has the structure of consciousness—that is, the "existence of continual self-negation"—but this process is only intuited, not grasped in the concept. Had Hegel pursued his definition of time as "Pure Being-within-itself as an absolute Coming-outside-itself," and had he attempted to think it through without the predetermined framework of his dialectic, he would have approached the same problem with which Nietzsche was grappling in his thought of eternal return.

In these sketchy remarks about the traditional treatment of the Self, we have seen that the problems of the Self and time converge more and more until they are inseparable. This is unquestionably connected with the increasing denial of substance. The philosophical issue at stake is no longer that of relating *res cogitans* to *res extensa*; it is that of thinking the Self as activity in its relation to the "world," a world which in its *meaning* can no longer be totally abstracted from the Self.

THE SELF AND ETERNAL RETURN

Nietzsche's statements about the Self in relation to eternal return are cryptic and difficult to understand. This is a problem which he never developed, never even fully communicated. Yet the fragments

---

[22] *Ibid.*, sec. 257; author's translation.
[23] *Ibid.*; author's translation.

which we have can serve as a basis for further thought and interpretation. These statements are largely to be found in the *Nachlass*, particularly in Volume XIV. Because these writings were not intended for publication, they lack the completeness and the polish of the published works; yet they point to the direction which Nietzsche intended to pursue and thus afford valuable insight into what he never fully accomplished.

I don't know how *I* came to this—but it is possible that the thought has come to me *for the first time*, the thought which splits the history of humanity into two halves. This *Zarathustra* is nothing but a preface, a preliminary hall—I have had to produce courage for myself since discouragement approached me from all sides: courage to *bear* that thought. For I am still far from being able to speak and describe it. *If it is true*—or rather, if it is believed to be true—then everything changes and turns around and *all* previous values are devalued.[24]

If the whole of *Zarathustra* is nothing but a preface, a prelude to the full communication of the thought of eternal return, then a dimension obviously remains which Nietzsche still felt incapable of portraying. One could say that Nietzsche is most *explicit* in his "scientific" investigations of eternal return. When the question of the *meaning* of eternal return for man arises, the element of mystery (enigma) prevails.

One of the main objections to a mechanistic interpretation of recurrence—that is, to recurrence as something automatic and predetermined—lies in Nietzsche's rejection of the idea that anything remains like itself or truly resembles anything else. The "sameness" of things is of our making; it is appearance which we have hypostasized as metaphysical truth.

The appearance of the empty (and the full), the firm (and the loose), the resting (and the moved), and the similar (and the dissimilar). Absolute space. Substance. The *oldest* appearance has been made into metaphysics. Human-animal standards of *certainty* are in there. Our *concepts* are inspired by our *poverty*.[25]

Taken on this "epistemological" (but never purely epistemological) level, the problem of the Same is intrinsically bound up with

24 Nietzsche to Overbeck, March 8, 1884; author's translation.
25 *Nachlass*, XIV: 20.

Nietzsche's rejection of Being in general. In a world of flux, or, more precisely formulated, in the world of the Will to Power, nothing is static. Neither the thinking and perceiving subject nor the apprehended object remains constant, not in relation to themselves or to each other. The dichotomy between (true) Being and (false) appearance, with which Nietzsche was incessantly concerned, is really not a dichotomy for him at all. Nietzsche argues that there is no static Being. Everything is appearance. There is no reality in itself. We ourselves are always active in the shaping of so-called reality. Therefore, what is supposedly real to us is actually "false."

That there is something like identical things, identical cases, is a basic fiction on the level of judgments, then on the level of conclusions.

Knowledge: the making possible of *experience* by a tremendous simplification of real events both on the part of the acting forces and on the part of our shaping forces: *so that there appears to be something like similar and identical things. Knowledge is falsification of the manifold and uncountable into the identical, the similar, the countable.* Thus *life* is possible only through such an *apparatus of falsification.* Thinking is a falsifying re-shaping; willing is a falsifying re-shaping. In all of this there lies the power of assimilation, which presupposes a will to make something like ourselves.[26]

If, however, static Being has no ontological status at all, it simply does not exist. Then there is no criterion by which one can judge appearance as false. If there is no Being, then there is also no appearance, in the sense of a distortion of that Being. The dichotomy collapses and we are left with the "actual occurrence."

What are the implications of these statements for the problem of the Same, or Self?

In traditional terminology the Self belongs to the subjective, the Same to the objective, side of the subject-object relationship. The Self is the core of the experiencing subject which persists through the multiplicity of that experience. The Same is the substance of the object persisting throughout the change of qualities or attributes. It is the principle of the identity of the object. The word "same," however, is broader and less exact than the word "self."

[26] *Ibid.,* 33, 69.

Self refers explicitly to a person, whereas the Same could be used to refer to anything self-identical, including a person.

The word "same" bears an immense and a precise significance in Nietzsche's thought. This significance is absolutely contextual—that is, the word "same" finds its meaning in the phrase "eternal return of the Same" and only in that phrase. Thus Nietzsche thinks the Same "verbally," from the dimension of eternal return. Whatever concept of the Self he had can be discovered only in the meaning of that phrase in its totality.

What is the basis for these assertions? It is at first a negative one: Nietzsche's radical rejection of the Self or the ego in any traditional sense. The most important passages dealing with the rejection of the Self are to be found in the section of the *Nachlass* volume entitled by its editors "The Will to Power as Knowledge."

Critique of modern philosophy: erroneous starting point, as if there existed "facts of consciousness"—and no phenomenalism in introspection.

Consciousness—to what extent the idea of an idea, the idea of will, the idea of a feeling (known to ourselves alone) are totally superficial! Our inner world, too, "appearance"!

Against positivism, which halts at phenomena—"There are only *facts*" —I would say: No, facts are precisely what there are not, only interpretations. We cannot establish any fact "in itself"; perhaps it is folly to want to do such a thing.

"Everything is subjective," you say; but even this is interpretation. The "subject" is not something given; it is something added and invented and projected behind what there is. Finally, is it necessary to posit an interpreter behind the interpretation? Even this is invention, hypothesis.

Insofar as the word "knowledge" has any meaning, the world is knowable, but it is *interpretable* otherwise; it has no meaning behind it, but countless meanings. "Perspectivism."

It is our needs that interpret the world, our drives and their For and Against. Every drive is a kind of lust to rule; each one has its perspective that it would like to compel all other drives to accept as a norm.

We set up a word at the point where our ignorance begins, at which we can see no further; for example, the word "I," the word "do," the word "suffer"—these are perhaps the horizon of our knowledge, but not "truths."

If there "is only one Being, the ego," and all other "Being" is fashioned after its model—if, finally, belief in the "ego" stands or falls with belief in logic—that is, the metaphysical truth of the categories of reason; if, on the other hand, the ego proves to be something in a state of Becoming: then—[27]

When one considers the historical interpretations of the Self outlined in the preceding section, one is forced to conclude that Nietzsche does not fit in with any of them. He does not, however, explicitly offer a new interpretation; rather, he offers negative statements about the Self. Nietzsche does not say what the Self is, he says what it is not. Is this tantamount to an absolute denial of any Self whatsoever? It is not. One could draw a somewhat superficial parallel here between "negative theology" and Nietzsche's "negative psychology." Nietzsche's statements move toward defining the Self by stating what it is not. This strengthens our assertion that the Self can be thought only in relation to eternal return. Had Nietzsche said that the Self was an ego, a subject, the Will, and so on, the Self could be interpreted as an entity independent of eternal return; at best, it would be something self-sufficient confronting the event of eternal return. This is not the case, however. Let us first examine Nietzsche's negative statements and then try to consider the problem of the Self within the context of eternal return.

The Self: Not a Subject or an Ego

The concept of the Self as a subject or as an ego is unacceptable to Nietzsche for two main reasons. The first main objection is found in Nietzsche's criticisms of the traditional concept of the Self, which he considers a *fiction*. The second main objection has its roots in the Will to Power. There is simply no basis whatsoever for a self in the traditional sense in a world which is the Will to Power and nothing else. These two objections are interrelated.

Many philosophers who emphasized the inner reality of the Self were faced with the problem of the ultimate reality, at least of the ultimate certainty and knowability, of the "outer" world. The outer world was appearance in one of the many senses of that word: either valid appearance for the inner self, appearance totally

[27] *The Will to Power*, 475, 476, 481, 482, 519.

dependent on that self, or else mere appearance, appearance in the sense of illusion. The two basic meanings of appearance are reflected here. Appearance can mean either the true appearance of something (as in "he appeared at the door"—that is, he could be seen—or "his appearance was disorderly"—that is, it really *was* disorderly) or else an illusory appearance (as in "he appeared to be happy," which implies that the appearance is superficial, that he really is not happy).

It is the sense of appearance as illusion which Nietzsche uses to characterize the traditional concepts of the Self.

> There exists neither "Spirit," nor reason, nor thinking, nor consciousness, nor soul, nor will, nor truth: all are fictions that are of no use. There is no question of "subject and object," but of a particular species of animal that can prosper only through a certain relative *rightness*; above all *regularity* of its perception (so that it can accumulate experience).[28]

This is a strong statement. Nietzsche obviously does not mean to deny any kind of consciousness whatsoever, but rather consciousness as a unity, as either a naïve or a transcendental unity. Above all, he denies that consciousness has an absolute substratum (subject) or is the cause of experience.

> The concept of *substance* is a consequence of the concept of the *subject*: *not* the reverse! If we relinquish the soul, "the subject," the precondition for "substance," disappears. One acquires *degrees of Being*, one loses that which has Being.

> Through thought the ego is posited; but hitherto one believed as ordinary people do, that in "I think" there was something of immediate certainty, and that this "I" was the given *cause* of thought, from which by analogy we understand all other causal relationships. However habitual and indispensable this fiction may have become by now —that in itself proves nothing against its imaginary origin—a belief can be a condition of life and *nonetheless* be *false*.[29]

In most of Nietzsche's criticisms of the Self either Descartes or Kant is tacitly in the background. As far as the connection between substance and subject is concerned, one is reminded here of

[28] *Ibid.*, 480.
[29] *Ibid.*, 485, 483.

Kant's statement that the feeling of permanence is necessarily constitutive for any experience whatsoever. Of course, Kant never said that the "I think" was the *cause* of experience; he merely stated that it must be able to accompany all experience. Nevertheless, the "I think" is the condition of all thought in that it is the transcendental unity of all experience. Without it experience could not be *my* experience. Even though Nietzsche is often not philologically exact with regard to the position of a particular thinker, he is almost always philosophically stringent with regard to the issue which concerns him.

Nietzsche is keenly aware of the presuppositions that go along with a concept of the Self. One cannot have an isolated concept of the Self without a knowledge of the fundamental concepts inextricably bound up with that Self. This is the dilemma of any *basic* philosophical problem.

One would have to know what *Being* is in order to decide whether this or that is real (for example, "the facts of consciousness"); in the same way, what *certainty* is, what *knowledge* is, and the like. But, since we do not know this, a critique of the faculty of knowledge is senseless: how should a tool be able to criticize itself when it can use only itself for the critique? It cannot even define itself![30]

Nietzsche uses the word "being" here in a sense unusual for him. He is not attacking being as static being, and he does not contrast it with becoming; rather, he uses it in the sense of reality, of what is real. The implication is that one must first know what being is, what is real, before one can understand the Self or more sophisticated problems such as certainty, knowledge, and a self-examination of the faculty of knowledge. Does this not put Nietzsche in a positivistic position? Is he not an absolute skeptic faced with bits and pieces of experience which have no unity, a skeptic unable to explain the how and what of knowledge—indeed, even denying the possibility and desirability of such an explanation?

According to Nietzsche, positivism (by this he means the positivism of his time) stops with the statement: "There are only *facts*." Nietzsche attacks positivism's metaphysical presupposition that facts are the ultimate, unquestionable reality beyond which

[30] *Ibid.*, 486.

one cannot go. "Fact" is an honorable and a solid word. No one disputes facts. But for Nietzsche these facts are the end products of unconscious interpretation. Yet there is no value judgment in his rejection of facts as ultimate realities. A world without facts is not a chaotic and unknowable world. It is simply a world where no independent, "objective" reality exists apart from human interpretation of that reality. This sounds somewhat like Kant, but, unlike Kant, Nietzsche has no universal subjectivity, no universally valid forms of sensibility and categories which structure experience. Kant states that the object must conform to our mental faculties, not vice versa. Nietzsche is not concerned with any such conformation. "Truth" for Nietzsche has little to do with the *adaequatio rei et intellectu.*

Truth is the kind of error without which a certain species of life could not live. The value for *life* is ultimately decisive.[31]

Truth has to do with life, not with the correspondence between a thought and its object. Life, however, is the Will to Power.

It is not possible to state simply that everything is subjective, however. This in itself is another interpretation, an interpretation claiming to state an objective fact. In order to say that everything is subjective, one would have to know what the subject is. For Nietzsche this is to fabricate an interpreter behind the interpretation, as in the fictional grammatical subject in the statement: "It is raining."

If the self is not an independent substance, can something "self-like" be based on one of the faculties of thought, perception, or will? The answer to this question will show that both thought and perception are subordinate to the Will to Power. They are the means by which the Will to Power attains certain goals, and thus are not ultimate.

The Will as a Possible Basis for the Self:
Will and the Will to Power

Nietzsche appears to have something in common with the empiricists in that he accepts perception as a basis for thought to a cer-

[31] *Ibid.,* 493.

THE SELF AND ETERNAL RETURN

tain extent. But perception is simply more immediate than thought; it is not more ultimate, for it, too, is the product of forming powers. Thus Nietzsche does not arrive at Hume's concept of the Self as a bundle of perceptions. These perceptions would not be basic enough to constitute a self and Nietzsche would probably be more interested in the "bundle," in what kept these impressions in some sense, however loose, together.

One would rather expect Nietzsche to base the Self on the will. If one accepts the Will to Power and eternal return as Nietzsche's two most fundamental thoughts, whatever Nietzsche means by the Self must have some basis in both. The relationship of these two thoughts is itself difficult to fathom, particularly since Nietzsche never expressed that relationship explicitly. Yet both thoughts are constantly present.

It is important to note that Nietzsche does not treat the Will to Power and eternal return in exactly the same manner. They lie, so to speak, in different dimensions. Thus one is not confronted with the statements "The world is the Will to Power," "The world is eternal return," and then faced with the problem of reconciling the two ideas with regard to the nature of the world. We shall return to this central problem after discussing the difference between the will and the Will to Power.

Does the basis for Nietzsche's concept of the Self lie in the will? If will is taken in its traditional meaning, the answer to this question is no. If will means the Will to Power, the answer is: to a certain extent. What is the difference between will and Nietzsche's concept of the Will to Power? Nietzsche arrived at his concept of the Will to Power through a constant grappling with, and increasing rejection of, Schopenhauer's concept of the will. In his earlier years Nietzsche was very much influenced by Schopenhauer's ideas and language. Whereas Schopenhauer's concept of the will is not the "traditional" concept, it is the concept against which Nietzsche is primarily negatively oriented. The prime reality in Schopenhauer's philosophy is the blind, suffering, needy will that seeks redemption in its appearances. Its seeking, however, is in vain. This will is basically a lack, and its efforts at release from its own incessant striving are thus doomed from the outset. In addition, the will is blind and can, strictly speaking, have no knowledge of its own efforts and goals, although Schopenhauer often speaks as if the will knew exactly what it was doing. This is one of the contradictory elements in Schopenhauer's thought, contradictory not in the sense of allowing genuinely unresolved problems to confront each other, as is often the case with Nietzsche, but contradictory in the sense of unclear thinking. A blind will does not know what it is striving for and is closer to "instinct" than to will in the traditional sense, which has always included thought.

Schopenhauer's concept of the will corresponds roughly to the revulsion or counter-will (*Gegen-Wille*) of which Nietzsche speaks in the chapter of *Zarathustra* entitled "Of Revenge." It is the will which still lies in chains, gnashing its teeth because it cannot will "against time." The will which is the Will to Power must will reconciliation with time, must will something still higher than reconciliation. The hidden relationship between time and power is expressed here.

The whole of Schopenhauer's philosophy aims at release from the will, achieved momentarily in the will-less contemplation of art or in what Schopenhauer calls "nirvana," by which he meant extinction. Nietzsche, however, regarded such a release from the will as (1) impossible and (2) a total misunderstanding of the meaning of life.

Schopenhauer's basic misunderstanding of the *will* (as if craving, instinct, drive, were the *essence* of will) is typical: lowering the value of the will to the point of making a real mistake. Also hatred against willing; attempt to see something higher, indeed that which is higher and valuable, in willing no more, in "being a subject without aim and purpose" (in the "pure subject free of will"). Great symptom of the *exhaustion* or the *weakness* of the *will*: for the will is precisely that which treats cravings as their master and appoints to them their way and measure.

Schopenhauer: we are something stupid and, at best, even something that cancels itself. Success of determinism, of the genealogical derivation of *obligations* that had formerly been considered absolute, the doctrine of milieu and adaptation, the reduction of will to reflexes, the denial of will as an "efficient cause"; finally—a real rechristening:

one sees so little will that the word becomes *free* to designate something else.[32]

Nietzsche's answer to the question of the denial of the will is
clearly stated in the *Genealogy of Morals:* "Rather will man will
Nothingness than not will." [33]

The fundamental trait of the Will to Power lies neither in the
nature of instinct or drive nor in that of consciousness. Instinct is
something less than will, for it is blind. Consciousness belongs to
the Will to Power, but only as a subordinate element, as an end
product. The essence of the Will to Power lies primarily in the
word "power."

It has been pointed out[34] that will and power in Nietzsche's
concept of the Will to Power are not two externally related components. Power is not something which the will lacks and after
which it strives as its external goal.

Is "will to power" a *kind* of "will" or identical with the concept
"will"? Is it the same thing as desiring? or *commanding*? Is it that
"will" of which Schopenhauer said it was the "in-itself" of things?

My proposition is: that the will of psychology hitherto is an unjusti-
fied generalization, that this will *does not exist at all*, that instead of
grasping the idea of the development of one definite will into many
forms, one has eliminated the character of will by subtracting from it
its content, its "whither?"—this is in the highest degree the case with
Schopenhauer: what he calls "will" is a mere empty word. It is even
less a question of a "will to live," for life is merely a special case of
the Will to Power; it is quite arbitrary to assert that everything strives
to enter into *this* form of the Will to Power.[35]

It is obvious that the Will to Power does not coincide with the
Will to Live. Nietzsche defines life itself as the Will to Power and
thus removes the possibility of defining the Will to Power in terms
of life, let alone the striving after life.

"Willing" is not "desiring," striving, demanding: it is distinguished
from these by the affect of commanding. There is no such thing as

[32] *Ibid.,* 84, 95.
[33] III: 28 and I: 1.
[34] Martin Heidegger, "Nietzsches Wort 'Gott ist Tot,'" in *Holzwege*
(Frankfurt: Klostermann Verlag, 1952).
[35] *The Will to Power,* 692.

"willing," but only a willing *something*: one must not remove the aim from the total condition—as epistemologists do. "Willing" as they understand it is as little a reality as "thinking": it is a pure fiction. It is part of willing that something is commanded (which naturally does not mean that the will is "effected"). That state of tension by virtue of which a force seeks to discharge itself is not an example of "willing."[36]

Two elements are fundamental for the Will to Power. One is the element of command, of mastery. Ultimately the highest command is command over oneself. This is intimately related to Nietzsche's statements in *Zarathustra* where Life repeatedly states: "I am that which must continually overcome itself." The other element is that of increase, of becoming More.

Unitary conception of psychology. We are accustomed to consider the development of an immense abundance of forms compatible with an origin in unity.

My theory would be: that the Will to Power is the primitive form of affect; that all other affects are only developments of it; that it is notably enlightening to posit *power* in place of individual "happiness" (after which every living thing is supposed to be striving)—"there is a striving for power, for an increase of power"; pleasure is only a symptom of the feeling of power attained, a consciousness of a difference (there is no striving for pleasure; pleasure supervenes when that which is being striven for is attained; pleasure is an accompaniment; pleasure is not the motive)—that all driving force is Will to Power; that there is no other physical, dynamic, or psychic force except this.

In our science, where the concept of cause and effect is reduced to the relationship of equivalence, with the object of proving that the *same* quantum of force is present on both sides, *the driving force is lacking*: we observe only results, and we consider them *equivalent* in content and force.

It is simply a matter of experience that change never ceases: we have not the slightest inherent reason for assuming that one change must follow upon another. On the contrary: a *condition once achieved* would seem to be obliged to preserve itself if there were not in it a capacity for desiring *not* to preserve itself.

Spinoza's law of "self-preservation" ought really to put a stop to change: but this law is false, the opposite is true. It can be shown

[36] *Ibid.*, 668.

most clearly that every living thing does everything it can *not* to preserve itself but to become *more*.[37]

According to Nietzsche, science, working with the concept of cause and effect, which simply describes an equation of forces, cannot explain the *working* force of events. This working force is the Will to Power and it includes all physical, dynamic, and psychic force. The Will to Power is not simply a natural force. In its fully developed form it includes the "higher" manifestations of consciousness. The living being does not strive for happiness; it strives for power, for the *More* in power. Joy is a symptom of attained power. It is consciousness of the difference brought about by attained power.

Life, as the form of being most familiar to us, is specifically a will to the accumulation of force; all the processes of life depend on this: nothing wants to preserve itself; everything is to be added and accumulated. . . . Life as a special case (hypothesis based upon it applied to the total character of Being) strives after a *maximal feeling of power*; essentially a striving for more power; striving is nothing other than striving for power; the basic and innermost thing is still this will. (Mechanics is merely the semeiotics of the results.)

If pleasure and displeasure relate to the feeling of power, then life must represent a growth in power, so that the difference caused by this growth must enter consciousness. If one level of power were maintained, pleasure would have only lowerings of this level by which to set its standards, only states of displeasure, not states of pleasure. The will to grow is of the essence of pleasure: that power increases, that the difference enters consciousness.[38]

The essence of the Will to Power lies neither in the sphere of instinct nor in that of consciousness. It includes and transcends both by striving to become More and by mastering this More in the grip of self-command.

What is the basis for the Self in the Will to Power? The answer to this question lies in a consideration of the Will to Power in its fully developed form. It points toward Nietzsche's concept of the higher man, the artist, and ultimately the superman. With the

[37] *Ibid.*, 688.
[38] *Ibid.*, 689, 695.

problem of the superman we come again to the thought of eternal return and to the question of the relationship of the Will to Power to eternal return.

The fore- and co-runners of Nietzsche's concept of the superman and of the higher type of human being in general are manifold. The monumental and the suprahistorical man in "The Uses and Disadvantages of History" (*Thoughts Out of Season*, number 3); the various types of the "higher man" in *Zarathustra*; the saint, the artist, and the ascetic priest in "What Do Ascetic Ideals Mean?" (*Genealogy of Morals*)—all are examples of a higher type of human being. We shall limit this discussion to Nietzsche's statements about the Will to Power as art and to the chapter in *Zarathustra* entitled "The Three Metamorphoses of the Spirit." The last polarity which Nietzsche arrives at is that of the last man and the superman. This polarity is a *true* polarity. Both poles remain. The superman is not the product of a pseudo-Darwinian evolution which would leave the last man behind. We shall return to this problem later on.

The Self and the Will to Power as Art

Art is for Nietzsche the highest form of human activity. In order to understand his treatment of the Will to Power as art, one must remember that for him art is not restricted to a particular sphere of human life, is not a collection of aesthetic objects and works; rather, it is the innermost nature of the world itself: "The world as a work of art that gives birth to itself." [39]

Nietzsche's "aesthetic" is based on the artist himself, not on the observer. It thus illuminates the nature of artistic activity rather than that of the aesthetic product. Art is understood in the broadest possible sense as a transfiguration and an affirmation of human existence.

It is a sign that one has turned out well when, like Goethe, one clings with ever-greater pleasure and warmth to the "things of this world": for in this way one holds firmly to the greater conception of man, that man becomes *the transfigurer of existence* when he learns to transfigure himself.

[39] *Ibid.*, 796.

What is essential in art remains its *perfection* of existence, its production of perfection and plenitude; art is essentially *affirmation, blessing, deification, of existence!*[40]

The artist shapes and transfigures not only his "material," what is to become his work; above all, he shapes and transfigures himself, and thus ultimately existence itself. Nietzsche is of course referring to the discipline necessary for the artist, as well as to the "creativity" of the artist in contrast to the "objectivity" of the scientist. But, beyond this, he points to a type of human being who *experiences* differently from the average man. This manner of experiencing is "active,"[41] not in the sense of arbitrary fabrication, but in the sense of being *able* to experience and shape a higher dimension of reality.

The questions with which Nietzsche was preoccupied all his life become thematic here: pessimism and tragedy, the classic and the romantic. These questions have their roots in the early work *The Birth of Tragedy*. They now re-appear in ripened form.

Romanticism: an ambiguous question, like everything modern. The aesthetic states twofold. The full and bestowing as opposed to the seeking, desiring.

Is art a consequence of *dissatisfaction with reality?* Or an expression of *gratitude for happiness enjoyed?*

What is romanticism? In regard to all aesthetic values, I now employ this fundamental distinction: I ask in each individual case, "has hunger or superabundance become creative here?" At first sight, another distinction might seem more plausible—it is far more obvious—namely, the distinction whether the desire for rigidity, eternity, *"Being,"* has been the cause of creation, or rather the desire for destruction, for change, for *Becoming*. But, when examined more closely, both kinds of desire prove to be ambiguous and interpretable according to the scheme mentioned above, which, I think, is to be preferred. The desire for destruction, change, Becoming, *can* be the expression of an overfull power pregnant with the future (my term for this, as is known, is the word "Dionysian"); but it can also be the hatred of the ill-

---

[40] *Ibid.*, 820, 821.
[41] This brings the artist close to active nihilism, which is a sign of the heightened power of the spirit, in contrast to passive nihilism, the decline and fall of the power of the spirit. See *ibid.*, 22.

constituted, disinherited, underprivileged, which destroys, *has* to destroy, because what exists, indeed existence itself, all being itself, enrages and provokes it. . . . "Eternalization," on the other hand, *can* proceed from gratitude and love—an art of this origin will always be an art of apotheosis, dithyrambic perhaps with Rubens, blissful with Hafiz, bright and gracious with Goethe, and shedding a Homeric aureole over all things—but it can also be that tyrannic will of a great sufferer who would like to forge what is most personal, individual, and narrow—most idiosyncratic—in his suffering into a binding *law* and compulsion, taking revenge on all things, as it were, by impressing, forcing, and branding into them this image, the image of his torture. The latter is romantic pessimism in its most expressive form, whether as Schopenhauerian philosophy of will or as Wagnerian music.

Whether behind the antithesis *classic* and *romantic* there does not lie hidden the antithesis active and reactive?[42]

Nietzsche makes a fundamental distinction between insufficiency, seeking, desire, and hunger, on the one hand, and gratefulness, fullness, overfullness, and giving, on the other. This distinction is not a purely "psychological" one. On the contrary, it is so fundamental that it undercuts the distinction between Being and Becoming as the aim of art.

The need for Becoming can lie in the Dionysian joy in the creation and destruction of individual forms. It can also lie in the rage and hate of the "small soul" driven to destroy anything which has attained the state of Being.

The need for Being can lie in an affirmative gratefulness for a state of being, in the wish to eternalize that state. It can also lie in the tyrannical will of the sufferer driven to take revenge on everything by stamping it with the mark of his own idiosyncratic torture.

In his reflective remarks about art in *The Birth of Tragedy*, Nietzsche again states that art is the authentic task of life, the *metaphysical* activity of life. Art is what makes life possible; it is the greatest stimulus to life. Only through art can all the tendencies of life-denial (religion, science) be overcome. Religion is nihi-

---

[42] *Ibid.*, 843, 845, 846, 847.

listic when it posits a "backworld,"[43] places all value and all reality in that world, and thus impoverishes "this" world, the only world. Science is nihilistic when it searches for the "truth," does not find the kind of truth it is searching for, and despairs over the discrepancy between life and truth.

Those overpowering artists who let a *harmony* sound forth from every conflict are those who bestow upon things their own power and self-redemption: they express their innermost experience in the symbolism of every work of art they produce—their creativity is gratitude for their existence.[44]

It is hardly possible to overestimate the importance of "art" in Nietzsche's thought. Art is not an isolated sphere of superfluous human activity originating in periods of leisure after the basic needs have been taken care of. Art is life, is the Will to Power in its full form. If the worm is in some sense more "basic" than the ninth symphony, it is hardly for this reason more "basic" in a different sense. Nietzsche's conception of art in *The Birth of Tragedy* ripens throughout his later writings, is gradually purged of the romantic elements of that work, and soon acquires a seriousness and a precision dictated by the scope of his experience.

How far does art reach into the inside of the world? And are there "artistic forces" apart from the "artist"? As one knows, this question was my *point of departure*: I said yes to the second question, and to the first, "The world itself is nothing but art!"[45]

In contrast to the scientific or the religious way of investigating or viewing life, Nietzsche arrives at a position very close to that of the pre-Socratic thinker Heraclitus, whom he always held in high esteem.

The phenomenon "artist" is still the most transparent: to see through it the basic instincts of power, nature, etc.! Also those of religion and morality! "Play," the useless—as the ideal of him who is overfull of strength, as "childlike." The "childlikeness" of God, *pais paizon*.[46]

[43] Nietzsche coined this expression as a caricature of the American "backwoods."
[44] *The Will to Power*, 852.
[45] *Nachlass*, XIV: 366.
[46] *The Will to Power*, 797. *Pais paizon*, "a child playing."

To Goethe

The Imperishable
Is only your image!
God, the insidious one
Is the surreption of poets . . .

World wheel, rolling,
Grazes goal upon goal:
The sulker names it—need,
The fool names it—play . . .

World Play, domineering
Mingles Being and Semblance
Eternal buffoonery
Mingles *us*, too! . . .[47]

Beyond causality, beyond goals and telos, even beyond Being and appearance, Nietzsche arrives at the World Play, the World Principle that cannot be fully explained, because it is beyond the power of human reason and human explanations. This World Principle is not irrational. We simply do not know the rules of the game.

The Self and the Superman

Before considering the extremely difficult question of the superman, we shall begin with the first chapter of *Zarathustra*, "The Three Metamorphoses of the Spirit." Nietzsche describes here the three metamorphoses that man must go through in order to attain the freedom necessary for original creativity. The spirit first becomes a camel, the load-bearing spirit. His motto is "you shall." The camel takes everything difficult and heavy upon himself. The meaning of his existence is to bear the load of all difficult things. He carries this load to the desert, where the second metamorphosis takes place.

In the desert the camel becomes a lion, the spirit of freedom and master of himself. His motto is "I will." The lion is no longer bound by the motto "you shall." He is free to overcome the sense of duty, to assume the freedom necessary for a new creativity, but he is not yet able actually to create new values.

[47] *The Joyful Wisdom*, "The Songs of Prince Vogelfrei"; author's translation.

86

The creator is the third stage of the spirit, the child. The motto of the child is "I am."[48] The child is "innocence and forgetfulness, a new beginning, a wheel which rolls out of itself, a first movement, a holy yea-saying."[49] This passage is compactly filled with expressions referring to Nietzsche's fundamental ideas. "Innocence" refers to the "Innocence of Becoming," a phrase which appears in the later works and above all in the many *Nachlass* plans for later writings. The Innocence of Becoming is a becoming free of guilt, free of its opposite, Being. When Becoming is judged by the standard of Being, it is devalued and judged as imperfect, as something which should not be. It can never reach the static standard of perfect Being.

"Forgetfulness" is reminiscent of Nietzsche's development of this concept in *The Uses and Disadvantages of History for Life*. There it is the necessary antidote to an overdeveloped historical consciousness, which kills action and life through the paralyzing knowledge of all that has been, through the feeling that everything that can be has already been.

The remaining phrases point to eternal return. A new beginning and a first movement point toward an uncaused beginning, a beginning with no past. The wheel rolling out of itself[50] expresses the same idea. This wheel is not the wheel of an automobile, a mere passive auxiliary of motion driven by an external force. It rolls out of itself. One is reminded here of Schubert, of the wheel of life incessantly and inevitably rolling as the musical undercurrent to the dramatic events occurring in his songs. In contrast to Schubert, however, for whom the uncanny element of this incessantly rolling wheel is prevalent, Nietzsche affirms the wheel's rolling out of itself as a holy yea-saying. The wheel *accompanies* Schubert as an undercurrent, whereas Nietzsche wants in some sense to become the wheel. The wheel of life loses its uncanny character of inevitable, incessant motion when it becomes a wheel rolling out of itself.

[48] See *The Will to Power*, 940.
[49] *Zarathustra*, "The Three Metamorphoses of the Spirit."
[50] See *ibid.*, I, "The Way of the Creating One" and "Child and Marriage."

We are now confronted with the question: What is the difference between the higher man, as depicted in *Zarathustra* and as foreshadowed in art, and the superman? What is still lacking in the higher man? What does he need in order to attain the superman? What is it that lifts the superman out of the dimension of all that has ever been and makes him something utterly unique? Strictly speaking, it is not possible to answer these questions, for the simple reason that there has not yet been a superman.

Never yet has there been a Superman. Naked have I seen both of them, the greatest man and the smallest man: All too similar are they still to each other. Verily, even the greatest found I—all too human![51]

Although many of Nietzsche's remarks seem to point to the possibility of "producing" a higher type of human being, they must be counterbalanced by a consideration of his polemic against Darwin and against the theory of the natural prevalence of higher types.[52] The gist of his arguments is that it is precisely the weak who prevail, not the "strong," and that there is no transition between types. The last man lives the longest.

Nietzsche's remarks about the struggle of the higher man against the bulwark of mediocrity have cultural validity and meaning, but they do not by any means exhaust the meaning of the superman.

The superman is indissolubly related to two main concepts of Nietzsche's thought: eternal recurrence and the death of God. This relationship can be simply stated as follows: The superman is the man who is able to affirm eternal recurrence, the man who experiences eternal recurrence as his own inner being. The superman is a possibility which appears with the death of God. The existence of the superman is apparently incompatible with the existence of God: "Dead are all the gods: Now do we desire the superman to live."[53] The superman is the goal of man; he is the most godlike being that humanity can reach.

This is an accurate restatement of Nietzsche's concept of the superman as set forth in *Zarathustra*. It is accurate, but oversimplified. We must ask what the "super" in the superman means.

[51] *Ibid.*, II, "The Priests."
[52] See *The Will to Power*, 684 and 685.
[53] *Zarathustra*, I, "The Bestowing Virtue."

Above what? Above the average man? This would amount to a feeble platitude, particularly when one considers the implications here of Nietzsche's concept of spirit (intellect) and body. Taking these two factors in man, in which would the superman excel? Certainly not in the intellect, for Nietzsche has strong reservations about the effect of the intellect on the development of man. The calculating intellect has often been more a hindrance than a furthering factor in man. This would leave us with the body. The superman would then be some kind of magnificent animal with more fully developed instincts and senses than those of man. This leads us no farther. How would such an animal be able to affirm eternal recurrence? The question obviously makes no sense. The superman is something above *man*, attained through the overcoming of *man*; and this overcoming could never lead back to some kind of "animal," to some kind of *"animal irrationale."*

If the superman cannot be primarily understood as a super-intellect or as a superanimal, the question then arises: Is the superman meant to be understood as an individual being or type at all?

Goal: to attain the superman for one moment. *For this* I suffer everything! [54]

This *Nachlass* fragment excludes the interpretation of the superman as an individual being. Here the superman is related to the individual as something which he attains as his goal. The implication is that of a higher *state* of man, a state constituted neither by a more fully developed intellect nor by a more fully developed body. This state lies beyond the fruitless dichotomy of intellect and body. In this sense, a sense which is alluded to only in a very general manner, the superman could be understood as something truly suprahuman, as opposed to the human, all-too-human.

Taken in isolation, Nietzsche's concept of the superman does not lead as far into a new dimension of thought as do his other main ideas. The superman has been open to a great deal of mis-interpretation. Some of this misinterpretation can even be "supported" by Nietzsche's own statements. To a certain extent the possibility of misinterpretation applies also to the Will to Power—for instance, when the Will to Power is understood primarily as a

[54] *Nachlass*, XIV: 306.

political force. It is perhaps only the concept of eternal return which is not open to such misinterpretation. Eternal return is such a strange idea that it can hardly even be misinterpreted.

In conclusion, a few remarks should be made about the relationship of the superman to the death of God. What Nietzsche meant by the death of God can be understood on different levels, but this meaning is basically clear. The levels are differentiated as follows:

1. The end of morality, the end of the ultimate distinction between good and evil.

2. The end of Christianity. But Christianity is basically "Platonism for the people"; thus, the end of Platonism (the distinction between Being and Becoming, between the other world and this world).

3. The end of the concept of an "existent ground" persisting throughout all change.

The third level, which is closely related to the second, is perhaps the most interesting of the three. A brief examination of what Nietzsche meant by an "existent ground" will lead us to the final section of this chapter: the relation of the Will to Power to eternal return.

Nietzsche's rejection of the other world, the Backworld, has already been discussed to some extent. This rejection also leads to his understanding of the relationship of truth to appearance and the distinction between a world of Being and a world of Becoming. How is the third implication of the death of God related to these fundamental problems?

The rejection of an existent ground of the world is perhaps even more basic than the rejection of the dualism of the world of Being and the world of Becoming. In the latter, Being is denied in the other world; in the rejection of an existent ground, Being is denied in *this* world—that is, all possible Being is denied. The connection between an existent ground and Being lies in the implications of the word "existent."[55] *Existent* does not mean simple existence, the fact that something is; rather, it means *unchangeable* existence and thus all the predicates that accompany unchangeableness— for instance, necessity.

[55] *Seiend.*

The rejection of an existent ground is the most "abstract" formulation of the death of God. "God" in this context is not a particularly religious concept; it is the general, philosophical concept of the ground of the world. Most philosophers have struggled with the problem of the relationship of the ground of the world to that world. Transcendence-immanence is the most basic polarity of the possibilities of that relationship. The ground of the world either transcends the world or is immanent in the world. Usually elements of both are necessary to explain the relationship; usually one factor predominates but does not exclude the other. If the ground of the world is absolutely transcendent to the world, it bears no relationship whatsoever to the world, and the problem arises: In what sense, then, is it the ground of the world? If the ground of the world is absolutely immanent in the world, then it simply coincides with the world and the word "ground" becomes superfluous. This would be the kind of superficial pantheism which adds up the number of constituents of the world and puts "God" after the equal sign. Even the philosopher perhaps closest to absolute immanence, Spinoza, never committed this sin of thoughtless oversimplification.

Nietzsche is certainly a philosopher of anti-transcendence. We stated in Chapter I that he rejected every concept related to transcendence except eternity. Had Nietzsche understood eternity as endless time, he would have been a philosopher of immanence in the absolute sense. It is more probable that Nietzsche was attempting to think the world in a manner which obviates the opposed possibilities of transcendence and immanence. In regard to the Will to Power he wrote:

The Will to Power: Attempt at a new interpretation of all occurrence.

With the rather dangerous title "The Will to Power" a new philosophy, or, more clearly expressed, *the attempt at a new interpretation of all occurrence* is to find expression.[56]

A new interpretation of all occurrence—that is what Nietzsche was striving for. Another name for this attempt is the innocence of

[56] *Nachlass*, XIV: 300–301.

Becoming, a becoming which is in no sense some kind of "fall" or derivation from an original state of Being.

The "how" of the death of God is a paradox; the "what" is relatively clear. The statement that man should be able to murder God, that the finite should be able to destroy the infinite, is in itself a paradox. A second paradox lies in Nietzsche's statement that we murder God and that God dies of his pity for man. More important than the "how," however, is the "what" of the death of God. What disappears with the death of God? The two main factors: an existent ground and a total collective knowledge of the world.

This is why all philosophers are instinctively trying to imagine a total consciousness, a consciousness involved in all life and will, in all that occurs, a "spirit," "God." But one has to tell them that precisely this turns life into a monstrosity; that a "God" and total sensorium would altogether be something on account of which life would have to be condemned—Precisely that we have *eliminated* the total consciousness that posited ends and means is our great relief—with that we are no longer *compelled* to be pessimists—*Our* greatest *reproach* against existence was the *existence of God*.[57]

Why does a total consciousness make existence a monster? A total consciousness, similar to the world of Being, makes existence superfluous by robbing it of its originality. Everything that could possibly happen in existence—past, present, and future—is already present in a total consciousness. Thus, whatever takes place in existence is a trivial repetition of what is already known. This total consciousness not only knows everything, it also observes everything. It is a kind of witness. The ugliest man in *Zarathustra*, the murderer of God, explains his deed:

But he *had* to die: he looked with eyes which beheld *everything*—he beheld man's depths and dregs, all his hidden ignominy and ugliness.

His pity knew no modesty; he crept into my dirtiest corners. This most prying, overintrusive, overpitying one had to die. He ever beheld *me*; on such a witness I would have revenge—or not live myself. The God who beheld everything, *and also man*: that God had to die! Man cannot *endure* it that such a witness should live.[58]

[57] *The Will to Power*, 707.
[58] *Zarathustra*, IV, "The Ugliest Man."

Why is the murderer of God the ugliest man? The ugliest man bears some similarity to the pale criminal,[59] the man who cannot bear the thought of his own deed once it is accomplished. He murders God in order to take revenge on this witness. Thus he falls prey to the most poisonous characteristic of life, revenge.[60] This makes him so ugly that even Zarathustra is overcome with pity and can hardly bear to look at him.

Nietzsche sees the innocence of all becoming in the fact that there is no being apart from the whole of becoming.

We others, who desire to restore innocence to becoming, would like to be the missionaries of a cleaner idea: that no one has given man his qualities, neither God, nor society, nor his parents and ancestors, nor he himself—that no one is to *blame* for him. There is no being that could be held responsible for the fact that anyone exists at all, that anyone is thus and thus, that anyone was born in certain circumstances, in a certain environment. It is a tremendous restorative that such a being is lacking. We are *not* the result of an eternal intention, a will, a wish: we are *not* the product of an attempt to achieve an "ideal of perfection" or an "ideal of virtue"—any more than we are a blunder on the part of God that must frighten even him (an idea with which, as is well known, the Old Testament begins). There is no place, no purpose, no meaning, on which we can shift the responsibility for our being, for our being thus and thus. Above all: no one could do it; one cannot judge, measure, compare the whole, to say nothing of denying it! Why not? For five reasons, all accessible even to the most modest intellects; for example, *because nothing exists besides the whole.* And, to say it again, this is a tremendous restorative; this constitutes the innocence of all existence![61]

The most basic fact of existence, of becoming, is that it has no possible final goal.

On the value of "becoming" . . . . To this end it is necessary to deny a total consciousness of becoming, a "God," to avoid bringing all events under the aegis of a being who feels and knows but does not *will*: "God" is useless if he does not want anything; moreover, this means positing a summation of displeasure and unlogic which would debase the total value of "becoming." Fortunately such a summarizing

[59] *Ibid.*, I, "The Pale Criminal."
[60] See Chapter I of this volume.
[61] *The Will to Power*, 765.

power is missing; a suffering and all-seeing God, a "total sensorium" and "cosmic spirit" would be *the greatest objection of being*. More strictly: one must admit nothing that has being.[62]

God, final goal, existent ground, Being—these are all different names for what Nietzsche seeks to exclude from existence: the finality of the unchangeable. One is reminded of his arguments for eternal recurrence when he states that, if a final state were possible, that would be the end of everything. If such a final state were reached, nothing could ever begin again, could ever be.

The Will to Power and Eternal Return

In this final section we shall try to clarify the difficult relationship between Nietzsche's two most basic concepts: the Will to Power and eternal return. Strangely enough, Nietzsche himself never related them explicitly. Metaphysically speaking, the rank of the Will to Power in Nietzsche's thought is clearer than that of eternal return. Nietzsche states: "Being—we have no idea of it apart from the idea of 'living.' How can anything dead 'be'?" Life, however, is the Will to Power. Thus one has by extrapolation the statement "Being is the Will to Power." Where does this leave eternal return?

In his interpretation of Nietzsche as the last thinker of Western metaphysics, Martin Heidegger places these two concepts in the basic framework of the essence-existence distinction of traditional metaphysics. The Will to Power is the essence, the "what" of the world; eternal return is the existence, the "how" and the "that" of the world. A full understanding of this interpretation depends upon an understanding of Heidegger's interpretation of the history of Western philosophy—that is, of metaphysics. A full discussion of his interpretation is not possible here, yet a few remarks might be made about the meaning of his view of the Will to Power and eternal return. The Will to Power could be understood as the essence of the world, if this essence were not seen as a static, general whole under which the individual entities of the world are to be subsumed. The Will to Power is the "what" of the world; it is what the world is. "This world is the Will to Power—and

62 *Ibid.*, 708.

nothing else. And you yourselves are this will to power—and nothing else!"[63]

The quotation comes from the conclusion of the *Nachlass* fragments entitled *The Will to Power*. But there are two versions of this conclusion. A comparison of the two will perhaps throw some light on the relation of the Will to Power to eternal return. The familiar conclusion is the second version, which emphasizes the Will to Power. The first version, printed in the notes to the volume *The Will to Power* in the *Grosse Oktavenausgabe*, emphasizes eternal return.

The beginning of fragment 1067, common to both versions, reads as follows:

And do you know what "the world" is to me? Shall I show it to you in my mirror? This world: a monster of force, without beginning, without end, a fixed, brazen quantity of force which grows neither larger nor smaller, which does not consume itself, but only transforms itself. As a whole its quantity is immutable, a household without loss and decrease, but also without increase, without gain, encompassed by "nothingness" as its limit. Nothing dispersed, wasted, nothing infinitely extended, but rather placed as definite force in definite space, and not in a space which might somewhere be "empty." Rather as force everywhere, as the play of forces and waves of forces at once one and many, here accumulating and at the same time there diminishing, a sea of forces storming and surging within themselves, eternally changing, eternally flowing back, with immense years of recurrence, with the ebb and flow of its forms. Driving from the simplest to the most complex, from the stillest, most fixed, coldest, into the most glowing, wildest, self-contradictory; and then again returning home from the fullness to the simple, from the play of contradictions back to the joy of consonance, affirming itself still in this sameness of its paths and years, blessing itself as that which must eternally come again; as a becoming which knows no satiety, no disgust, no fatigue: this my *Dionysian* world of eternal self-creation, eternal self-destruction, this mysterious world of twofold voluptuousness, this my "Beyond good and evil," without a goal. . . .

Version two continues:

Unless a goal lies in the happiness of the circle, without will, unless a ring has good will toward itself,—do you want a *name* for this world?

[63] *Ibid.*, 1067.

A *solution* for all of your enigmas? A *light* for you, too, you most concealed, strong, undaunted midnight ones? *This world is the Will to Power, and nothing else!* And you yourselves, too, are this Will to Power—and nothing else!

Version one continues:

. . . unless a ring is willing to revolve always around itself and only around itself on its own path: This is *my* world—who is awakened enough to look at it without wishing blindness for himself? Strong enough to hold his soul up to this mirror? To hold his own mirror up to the mirror of Dionysus? And would not whoever could do this have to do still more? Would he not have to pledge *himself* to the "ring of rings"? With the pledge of his own *return?* With the ring of eternal self-blessing, self-affirmation? With the will to will again and yet again? To will back all things which have ever been? To will outward to everything that will ever have to be? Do you know now what *the world* is for me? And do you know what *I* will when I will *this world?*[64]

The first version ends, not with "this world and you yourselves are the Will to Power and nothing else," but with "Do you know what I will when I will this world?" To will this world cannot mean simply to accept the status quo of the world as it is and then to "will" it. Nietzsche's question is, What is it that I will when I will this world? The unpublished version emphasizes eternal return and thus questions precisely the "what" of the Will to Power. It recalls the *enigma* of *Zarathustra* and stresses the relation of the soul's solution to the enigma of Dionysus. This "solution" does not take the form of finding an ultimate, changeless "answer." He who finds the "solution" must do still more. He must pledge himself to the "ring of rings," and this pledge involves "the will to will again and yet again." The crucial question at stake here is whether or not the nature of this "willing" coincides completely with the traditional definition of the term. If so, then Heidegger's interpretation of eternal return as existence and the Will to Power, ultimately conceived of as the Will to Will, as the essence of the world, would tend to fit Nietzsche's statements. In any case, there is much to be said for Heidegger's interpretation of Nietzsche as

[64] *Ibid.*; author's translation.

the last figure of metaphysics. But, if there is a dimension of eternal return which cannot be completely explained by, or subordinated to, the Will to Power, one might look for some element in Nietzsche which not only represents the completion of metaphysics but also contains the seeds of a new way of thinking.

In some of his writings,[65] Heidegger seems at times to hesitate to set eternal return totally within the framework of metaphysics as the existence of the world, emphasizing instead the enigmatic nature of Nietzsche's abysmal thought, that element which cannot be understood by metaphysical thinking.

The element of will is undoubtedly strong in Nietzsche's thinking. This he shares with the philosophical tradition since the beginning of Christianity and particularly with the nineteenth century, above all with Schelling.[66] If there is anything new about Nietzsche's concept of the Will to Power, it is to be found in the idea of *power*. Because the phrase "Will to Power" does not mean will as a striving after something external to that will ("power"), the meaning of power is crucial and intrinsic to understanding what Nietzsche meant by the will itself.

Nietzsche worked out his concept of the Will to Power in a constant polemical struggle against Schopenhauer's concept of the Will to Live. Apart from his objections to the idea of a will to *live*, Nietzsche objected to the quality of *lack*, of blind, needy, suffering, and insatiable striving in Schopenhauer's concept. Speaking of Schopenhauer, Nietzsche wrote:

Only he did not understand how to *make* this will *godlike*: he got stuck in the moral-Christian ideal. Schopenhauer was still so far under the dominion of Christian values that, when the thing-in-itself was no longer "God" for him, he had to see it as bad, stupid, absolutely objectionable. He did not comprehend that there can be infinite ways of being-able-to-be-other, even of being-able-to-be-God.[67]

Apart from the fact that Nietzsche believed that Schopenhauer completely misunderstood the nature of will, the criticism here is

---

[65] Particularly in "Who is Nietzsche's Zarathustra?" *Review of Metaphysics*, 20, no. 3 (1967).

[66] See *Of Human Freedom* (Chicago: Open Court, 1936), where Schelling says that all primal being is will.

[67] *The Will to Power*, 1005.

that when Schopenhauer could no longer find the positive values of Christian morality in the Will to Live, he simply posited all of the "negative" values of that morality as belonging to the will. Schopenhauer's will, or "God," or "Being," is something bad, stupid, absolutely objectionable. Nietzsche, however, wants to think "beyond good and evil." This does not mean that he wants a total anarchy of arbitrariness; rather, he wants to go beyond a certain kind of value judgment. To go beyond the value judgments "this is good," "this is evil," whereby the things thus valued are *fixed* with these predicates, does not really mean to abolish completely the ideas of good and evil, but rather to put them in their *perspective*. They are not ultimate. If taken as ultimate, they can blind us to the nature of things as they are and as they can be.

The concept of value is a highly complex one in Nietzsche's thought. On the one hand, he wants to overcome traditional morality and valuing,—above all, Christian morality. On the other hand, he makes constant use of the concept of value in connection with the Will to Power, which posits values after which it strives. Nietzsche never clearly distinguishes the nature of this non-moral *valuing* from the moral values he constantly attacks. With his idea of the transvaluation of all values, undoubtedly a basic concept of his later writings, he gets stuck in the framework of valuing and value judgment, which makes of that aspect of his philosophy a peculiar kind of extreme subjectivism.

Nietzsche does say, however, that valuing is creating, and it is this statement which we shall pursue further, for it provides the link between the Will to Power and art. When one understands valuing as creating and art, one gains further insight into what Nietzsche meant by power in the Will to Power. An understanding of power leads ultimately to a fuller comprehension of what he meant by "being," or "God." "Under the not undangerous title 'The Will to Power,' a new philosophy, or, spoken more clearly, *the attempt at a new interpretation of all occurrence*, should come to word." [68] The phrase "a new interpretation of all occurrence" makes one question whether the Will to Power can be equated with an essence or "what" of the world.

[68] *Nachlass*, XIV, 418.

If all will is not to be equated with the revulsion against time and its "it was"—which always remains a possibility, but never an inherent necessity—it has possibilities other than getting caught in the backward-directed teeth-gnashing of revenge. The will that is freed from revenge strives for a maximal feeling of power.

Life as a single instance (from here the hypothesis about the total character of existence) strives for a *maximal feeling of power*; is essentially a striving for a more of power; striving is nothing other than striving for power; the deepest and innermost of all is this will.[69]

Nietzsche's new discovery of power makes him feel that he has discovered a totally new concept of will: "Finally—a real rebaptism: one sees so little of will that the word becomes *free* to name something else."[70]

Whereas Schopenhauer believes that the will is something absolutely objectionable, Nietzsche goes off in search of infinite ways of being-able-to-be-other, of being-able-to-be-God. This search takes him into the realm of art. "Our religion, morals, and philosophy are forms of the decadence of man. The *countermovement: art.*"[71]

The phenomenon of power is shown most clearly in Nietzsche's analyses of beauty and the great style. In beauty and in the great style, opposites are united under the yoke of form to produce an intensity without tension, and this is the feeling of power. The great style is an "expression of the 'Will to Power itself'";[72] it is the "culmination of development."[73]

Thus Nietzsche analyzes power in its manifestations in art and in the great man, and then goes on to say that, if anywhere, it is in the phenomenon of power that the non-moral affirmation of the will (in Schopenhauer's language), or "God," is to be found. "The only possibility of maintaining a meaning for the concept 'God' would be: God not as driving force, but God as maximal state, as an ἐποχή."[74]

[69] *The Will to Power*, 689.
[70] *Ibid.*, 95.
[71] *Ibid.*, 794.
[72] *Ibid.*, 341.
[73] *Ibid.*, 800.
[74] *Ibid.*, 1035.

With the word ἐποχή ("epoch") Nietzsche defines power as a "holding to itself," a "checking itself." This checking is not related to any kind of external hindrance blocking the Will to Power. It is a self-checking,[75] a self-ruling. Instead of thinking God as the initiator of the world or as its driving force, Nietzsche thinks God as the maximal state or, as expressed in another passage, as the moment of culmination. "'God' as moment of culmination: existence is an eternal becoming and disappearance of the godlike. *But, in this, no highpoint of value*, but a highpoint of *power*."[76] And finally: "God the highest power—that is enough! From it follows everything, from it follows—'the world'!"[77]

Nietzsche never elaborates on the question of how the world "follows" from God. His non-polemical statements about God are so sparing that one can do little more than reflect on them; seldom is one able to arrive at any comprehensive theory. In one passage, however, Nietzsche does characterize this relationship of following as "around": "Around the hero everything becomes tragedy, around the demigod everything becomes satyr-play; and around God everything becomes—what? perhaps 'world'?"[78] This passage suggests the image of a center of power from which the world, so to speak, radiates. It seeks to describe the "ring of rings" in its aspect of power and what follows from that power. It is also reminiscent of the "wheel rolling out of itself."

In conclusion, we return to the question of the relationship of the Will to Power to eternal return. If the Will to Power is thought primarily in terms of the concept of power, and if one does not forget Nietzsche's concept of the innocence of becoming, which belongs to the manner of development of the Will to Power, then the Will to Power is closely related to eternal return, but is not the essence of the world, whose existence is eternal return. The innocence of becoming means that nothing is intended by becoming. Becoming is not there for any purpose; rather, it is self-justifying, if one wants to speak of justification here at all.

[75] The English word "check" is etymologically related to the word "power."
[76] *The Will to Power*, 712.
[77] *Ibid.*, 1037.
[78] *Beyond Good and Evil*, 150.

Nietzsche states that, if there is no aim or goal in the world process, affirmation is possible; something is attained in that process in every moment, and it is always the Same. The attainment of the Same in every moment is what he calls a God beyond good and evil.

Thus the link between power and God, or what Nietzsche calls his kind of "pantheism," provides a clue to the relationship of the Will to Power to eternal return. Nietzsche's "pantheism" does not say "God is everywhere" or "God is everything"; rather, it emphasizes that God is in every moment. This is a "temporal" determination of God, or power, temporal not in the sense of making God finite but as a way of thinking that is not spatial.

If the Will to Power is in any sense the "what" of the world, it is the "what" in that it is the last *fact* at which we can arrive.[79] The Will to Power is, so to speak, the givenness of the world. This brings it closer to the existence of the world, in the sense of what is *there*, than to its essence, or *what* is there. Nietzsche's treatment of eternal return, on the other hand, wavers between regarding it also as a kind of facticity and questioning it as the freedom of radical possibilities of being. In the latter emphasis eternal return is regarded as a *thought*, not as a fact. The fundamental meaning of the word "thought" here is not that of an idea *about* something existent. "Thought" points to the possibility of transformation through root awareness.

Without eradicating the differences between Nietzsche's two fundamental concepts, and without fitting them into the framework of a systematic relationship which Nietzsche never reached and perhaps did not wish to reach, one might say that the Will to Power is the world considered as "—and nothing else!" and that eternal return is the world considered as "This is *my* world, the ring of rings to which I pledge my *own* return." Whoever is strong enough to hold up his own mirror and solution to the mirror and the enigma of Dionysus will experience "a joyous affirmation (of the Dionysian) as the total character of life, as that which is the same in all change, the same as the equally powerful, the equally blissful."[80] The Will to Power emphasizes the facticity of the

[79] *Nachlass* (Kröner ed.), vol. 83, p. 288.
[80] *The Will to Power*, 1050.

world. Eternal return offers the possibility of a joyous affirmation of the "Same" in that world. This "same," the sameness of power and bliss in the total character of life, is Nietzsche's experience of the Self. It is the meeting of "my *own* return" with "the ring of rings."

Who are you, my soul? . . . oh, heaven above me, . . . when will you drink this strange soul—when, well of eternity! you serene, awesome abyss of midday! When will you drink my soul back into yourself?[81]

[81] *Zarathustra*, IV, "Midday."

IV

TIME AND
ETERNAL RETURN

ETERNAL RETURN AND
TRADITIONAL THEORIES OF TIME

The most obvious thing to do in interpreting Nietzsche's thought
of eternal return is to think of this return within the framework
of cycles of "time." This procedure is so obvious that it is very
difficult to think of eternal return in any other way. The attempt
will now be made, however, to think eternal return, not within the
framework of pre-existing cycles, but as the "occurrence" of time
itself.

Two things about this attempt should be stated at the outset.
(1) The attempt follows up one of the possibilities offered by
Nietzsche's thought—that is, the possibility which is opposed to
eternal recurrence in its nihilistic form.[1] Using the distinction between recurrence and return made in this study but not explicitly
by Nietzsche, one could say that the attempt follows up the idea
of return as opposed to a mechanistically thought recurrence. (2)
This attempt is admittedly an interpretation and is forced to "go
beyond" Nietzsche's writings, published or unpublished, on the

[1] See pp. 16–21.

subject of eternal return. If one adheres strictly to what Nietzsche wrote about eternal return, it is impossible to "solve" the enormous problems inherent in this thought. It is impossible to "solve" this thought neatly in any case, for it remains *in essence* enigma as well as vision. Even its aspect of vision, of something seen, cannot be exhaustively ordered into a pat conceptual framework.

If, as Nietzsche describes in *Ecce Homo*, eternal return is something which *invaded* him, one might say that he was overcome by something which he did not and could not fully comprehend. This would help to explain the many contradictions that abound in his statements about eternal return. The contradictions are, however, fruitful. They represent partial aspects which Nietzsche was unable to integrate into a larger "whole," to some extent because he had renounced any kind of "synthesis," which is a mark of dialectical thinking. In addition, some of the contradictory aspects of eternal return are contradictory possibilities of being. They have to do with a unique kind of "existential choice," and not with the criterion of a logical system, self-consistency.

It is not possible within the scope of this study to go into a detailed analysis of the traditional theories of time. We must be content to pick out the most basic characteristics common to these theories at the price of oversimplification. Perhaps the most basic thing which these theories share is the idea of time as *"in time."* Everything that we know is *"in time"*: trees, animals, stones, man. To be in time means to be thrown into a process which is irreversible, a process which ultimately takes everything out of existence just as it presumably brought things into existence. Hegel states that things begin to die as soon as they are born. Time is an absolute, inexorable framework in which everything is, a framework which is not indifferent to what is in it, but which somehow inexplicably "causes" everything in it to perish. How such an indifferent framework can affect its "content" has never been a central question in Western philosophy. If this devouring quality of time is essential to time, the idea of persisting throughout "all time" is nonsensical. It is incompatible with the nature of time.

A simplistic interpretation of Nietzsche's thought of eternal return might read: everything, including man, is born, lives its life, dies, and in some unfathomable way is reborn. Time moves in continuous cycles, bringing everything back again in repetition.

What if time did not do this? What if there were no absolute framework of time within which things were born, lived, died, and were reborn? What if there were no *extended* stretch of time always "there" as the foundation upon which everything occurs— indeed, as a guarantee of the possibility or even the necessity of the occurrence? For example, if I think, "next month I shall take a vacation," I express the belief that there is a continuous stretch of time leading up to that day next month when I shall go on vacation. The stretch of time "leads up" to that day by *elapsing*. If the stretch of time did not elapse, the day of my vacation would never "come." But I "know" that it will come. And precisely this inexorable coming, which is a coming-to-pass in the double sense of actually happening and inevitably passing away, will bring all that is in store for me, ultimately my death. I cannot go backward in time. I cannot get out of time. I am caught in it, living in an irreversible direction.

This way of thinking about time applies equally well to the basically Christian concept of historical, "directed" time, which has a beginning, a middle, and an end, and to the Greek and to most of the Eastern (particularly the Indian) concepts of cycles of time repeating themselves.

What would happen to the thought of eternal return if one took away this framework of time? There would be no absolute duration between birth and death. "Recurrence," or return, would take place in an instant, in every instant. Without this framework of time, the whole meaning of birth and death themselves would be challenged.

Such a possibility did occur to Nietzsche, but only in fragmentary, momentary insights, the implications of which he was unable to think through in connection with the whole. For example, it occurred to him with reference to the "interval" between death and rebirth.

You think you have a long rest until rebirth—but do not fool yourselves! Between the last moment of consciousness and the first appearance of new life lies "no time"—it passes by like a stroke of lightning, even if living creatures measure it in terms of billions of years or could not measure it at all. Timelessness and succession are compatible as soon as the intellect is gone.[2]

One of the experiences which negated the framework of time for Nietzsche was the experience of timelessness. In two chapters of *Zarathustra*, "Midday" and "The Drunken Song," Nietzsche describes Zarathustra's experience of this "no time." Zarathustra says:

What happened to me: Listen! Did time not fly away? Am I not falling? Did I not fall—listen! into the well of eternity? What is happening to me? Still! . . . When, well of eternity, you serene terrible abyss of midday, when will you drink my soul back into yourself?"[3]

In the chapter entitled "Midnight," Zarathustra again says, "Where did time go? Did I not sink into deep wells?"[4]

Zarathustra experiences here an "eternity" which has nothing to do with an endless persistence in some transcendent realm. Eternity is compared to a well. It is, so to speak, the "purely vertical" experienced with a kind of vertigo which results from the sudden release from the horizontal connection of successive time. Zarathustra "falls" into this well; the abyss of midday drinks his "soul" back into itself. "Midnight is also midday." They are the "same." Midday emphasizes the blinding flash of lightning striking consciousness; midnight emphasizes the dark, deep well reabsorbing that consciousness.

These experiences "embody" the "answers" to the questions posed by Nietzsche in the first version of the end of *The Will to Power*.

Who is strong enough to hold his own mirror up to the mirror of Dionysus? His own solution up to the enigma of Dionysus? And would not whoever could do that have to do still more? Would he not have to pledge *himself* to the "ring of rings"? With the pledge of his own return?[5]

[2] *Nachlass* (Kröner ed.), vol. 83, no. 1341.
[3] *Zarathustra*, IV, "Midday."
[4] *Ibid.*, "The Drunken Song."
[5] *Nachlass*, XVI: 315.

Enigma and vision have become here enigma and "solution." This "solution" is no mere theoretical "answer" to an intellectual puzzle. It is the literal *release* (in the sense of *solvere*) *into* that enigma itself. Holding one's own solution up to the enigma of Dionysus results in pledging *oneself* to the ring of rings, in pledging one's own return, not to the world of endlessly repeated cycles, but into the abyss of "eternity," which is the ring of rings.

This is not a bold thought. It is an incredibly radical experience, an experience so radical that Nietzsche himself was unable to maintain the purity of the dimension we have described here as the "vertical." He sought "to will back all things which have ever been," thus dispersing this vertical dimension back into the horizontal, back into the realm of "all things knotted so closely together," back to the causal chain of mechanistically conceived things and events "in time." It is not time that is a circle, as the dwarf would have us believe; it is eternity which is the ring of rings, the ring being thought of here as the absolute rejection of mechanistically *or* teleologically conceived time. There is no teleology involved in the ring, and there is no mechanistic determinism either. The ring of rings circles back into itself; its whole being is return. There is no substance, no "God" in the Christian sense. There is "God" only as the highest *power* from which "follows" the world. Nietzsche was able to glimpse eternity as sheer occurrence, not as static persistence. Eternity *is* eternal return of the Same. The Same is not a thing or a person recurring in endless cycles of absolute time. The Same *is* return. Return can "occur" only in the moment. It can never be constituted by durational cycles, for these cycles never meet, never produce a return; they are only endless, meaningless recurrence.

Thus we have the significance of the Moment. The Moment is not an isolated instant somehow lifted out of the chain of temporal succession. The question of how the Moment is related to the "rest" of time turns out to be a spurious one. Only what is extended, extended also in the sense of enduring and remaining, can be "related" as one thing is to another. The Moment does not relate to the rest of time, because the rest of time never *is* in the sense of persistence. The Moment "relates" to every moment in such a way that one moment *is* every moment.

If only one moment of the world came back—spoke the lightning flash—all must come back.[6]

Can we remove the idea of purpose from the process and still affirm the process? That would be the case if something within that process were *attained* in every moment—and always the same. . . .

Every fundamental characteristic which underlies every event, which expresses itself in every event, would have to drive the individual to affirm triumphantly every moment of existence in general, if the individual experienced it as *his* fundamental characteristic.[7]

Not only can one remove the idea of purpose from the process and still affirm the process, the "process" can be affirmed *only* when the idea of purpose is removed, when the innocence of becoming is attained. Teleology is also a form of causality; it also leads to "all things being firmly knotted together." Freed of any kind of causality, teleological or mechanistic, something can be attained at every moment—and always the Same.

Nietzsche's strange word "Same" (*das Gleiche*) turns out to *be* only in and as return in every moment. It is not a "content" in any possible sense of that word. It is not a "what" at all, but a movement: the incalculable, inexhaustible movement of eternal return. All of Nietzsche's insight into the lack of substance, subject, substratum, "Being," and so on, culminates in this thought. Substance, subject, substratum, and Being are all hidden forms of the "persisting ground," the double figure of substance and causality which is the *hindrance* to eternal return because it prevents any possible originality of occurrence. The spirit of revenge which struggles against the "it was" must be overcome. Redemption from revenge consists in winning back the innocence of becoming, in freeing becoming to be sheer occurrence with no obstruction.

I teach you release from the eternal flow; the stream flows back into itself again and again, and you enter the same stream again and again, as the Same.[8]

The release *from* the eternal flux is really release *into* the again and again of that eternal flux.

---

[6] *Ibid.* (Kröner ed.), vol. 83, no. 1358.
[7] *The Will to Power*, 55.
[8] *Nachlass* (Kröner ed.), vol. 83, no. 1300.

One must want to perish in order to be able to come into being again, from one day to the next. Metamorphosis through a hundred souls—let that be your life, your fate![9]

When the thought of eternal return is freed from the dichotomy of time as a *form* in which some indifferent "content" occurs and recurs, a possibility is opened up—that of thinking of eternal return as the relation of time to eternity.

The Traditional Relation of Time to Eternity

We stated in Chapter I that there are four basic conceptions of eternity: (1) endless duration, (2) the eternal present (*nunc stans*), (3) the simultaneity of all the disparate, successive moments of time, and (4) timelessness. Some aspects of these conceptions overlap. For example, an eternal present is also "timeless" in that it is somehow removed from the flux of time. Yet these two concepts do not coincide, for the meaning of *presence* is lacking in the concept of timelessness.

One might say that the two most basic (traditional) characteristics of time as a whole are the flow of time and its character as form (the "in time" already mentioned). For the moment we are bracketing the question of the articulation of time into past, present, and future, for these have never been thought in a way that could essentially alter or even affect the two characteristics of time as a whole. Rather, the articulation of time has been subordinated to the two characteristics of time as a whole. This is not to say that it is more desirable to constitute the whole of time, starting from its more "original" articulations or parts. Time can be thought neither as parts constituting a whole nor as a general whole from which parts can be derived and divided up. The schema whole-part, or universal-individual, is inadequate for an understanding of time. It is even incommensurable with that understanding.

The meaning of the flux or flow of time lies in its character of passing away, taking all along with it and thus effecting the perishability of all things. The meaning of time as a form ("in time")

---

[9] *Ibid.*, no. 1299.

lies in its restricting character with regard to experience (Kant, Schopenhauer), or, more fundamentally, in its character of inescapability. Things are "caught" in time. They are not in the flux occasionally or by chance. Things in time are moving inexorably toward decay and death. Time's quality of passing away brings everything to ultimate extinction with no reprieves and no exceptions.

Each of the four above-mentioned conceptions of eternity in some way represents an overcoming of the "negative" quality of time. Eternity must always be in some way "related" to time if it is to preserve any independent meaning of its own as compared with the corresponding metaphysical concepts of Being, the One, and so on. The crucial question here concerns the nature of this relationship. After briefly examining the relation of time to eternity implicit in these four conceptions of eternity, we shall question the possibility of some other kind of relation, a possibility suggested, but never developed, by Nietzsche's thought of eternal return.

Eternity as endless duration is the simplest and also the least adequate of the four concepts. It is completely oriented toward the concept of duration and it totally ignores time's quality of passing away. It is purely quantitative. Eternity in this sense is the endless prolongation of duration as we presumably experience it. Strangely enough, this concept of eternity lies very close to Nietzsche's thought of eternal return in its nihilistic form (duration with an "in vain"). Endless duration in itself is not sufficient to guarantee an "affirmative" concept of eternity. On the contrary, it could mean the exact opposite. For example, the fate of Sisyphus involves endless duration. Endless duration is purely "formal," in the sense that everything depends on the "content," on what is going on in that duration, and on the possible existence of something meaningful and purposive. When it is more deeply thought out, there is something almost appalling about endless duration. If thought as a kind of insatiable, unendable necessitation to continue on and on, it borders on the demonic.

The negative quality of time which is overcome by this concept is simply the quantitative limit of a stretch of time. If a limited stretch of time could be infinitely prolonged, finitude would be overcome.

The eternal present (*nunc stans*) is perhaps the most comprehensive and fruitful of the four concepts of eternity. It embodies the idea of presence, a presence excluding past and future and thus all the negative qualities of time here conceived of as absence. The past is no longer; the future is not yet. The eternal present is a present which never ceases to be present. If there were a time when it had not been attained, when it presumably was not yet, this time would bear no essential relationship to it. The eternal present would simply be not yet realized, but it would be potentially "there," waiting to be attained. Its "absence" is not really a lack, but only a being hidden. It is not yet experienced or discovered, but it is potentially present. Once attained, it can never be lost, never become past.

By implication the eternal present contains the essential aspects of simultaneity and timelessness. It is timeless insofar as it is changeless and never passes away. It ought to involve some kind of simultaneity of the modes of time if it is not to be thought as a relationless, atomistic moment of time. Otherwise it excludes the past and the future, and the problem of the relation of one moment to every moment becomes the insoluble opposition of one moment of time to all the "rest" of time. In other words, the "in every moment" becomes impossible because the one moment absolutized and rigidified excludes any possibility of continuing occurrence.

The negative quality of time which the eternal present overcomes is the "absence" inherent in the past and the future. This conception of eternity is genuine in that it emphasizes the quality of presence without which eternity could not be thought, but it is forced to think this presence or now as "standing," as static in contradistinction and opposition to the flux of time.

Eternity as the simultaneity of past, present, and future expresses wholeness and totality. Perhaps the best example of this simultaneity is the idea of a developing process which unfolds successively what is in itself enveloped and all at once. Hegel is perhaps the archprotagonist for this concept. Despite his repeated assertions that the Absolute is *result*, that absolute is in its absoluteness (in

111

its transcendence and self-being) "simultaneously present." Nothing occurs in the unfolding world process which is not present in the eternal, simultaneous Absolute. In Hegel's system there is no possibility of essential occurrence which is extraneous to the Absolute Spirit. The world process is simply the development of what is simultaneously present in the Absolute. Without the self-being of simultaneous presence, the Absolute would be dispersed into the moments of its development and lose itself in sheer immanence.

Eternity as the simultaneity of past, present, and future overcomes the successiveness of time. Successiveness harbors the possibility of loss and dispersion. If thought directionally, successiveness means the procession of all things following each other into the past. Even in the past their character of disparateness cannot be overcome. They remain successive, not integral. Only simultaneity can overcome successiveness. More precisely, only simultaneity can prevent successiveness. But, in thinking this simultaneity, it is very difficult to avoid placing it *next to* the process of which it is the simultaneity and thus seriously jeopardizing its self-dynamic quality.

Eternity as timelessness expresses unchangeability. Where there is no time, there can be no change. This conception of eternity bears no positive relation to time. It is related to time negatively, by exclusion, which involves, logically speaking, a dependency, but not genuine relation. Timelessness overcomes time's quality of change, but it is open to the criticism of being static and lifeless. It is a purely negative (in the sense of the *via negationis*) conception and has no concrete meaning.

The Significance and Implications of Nietzsche's "There Is No End" for a Theory of Time

Despite all the problems, contradictions, and diverse possible interpretations of Nietzsche's thought of eternal return, one thing about it is indisputable. Its basic meaning, stated in a neutral fashion, is that there is no finality. This lack of finality embraces this world, as well as any possible "transcendence." With reference to transcendence, lack of finality simply means that there is no final, static ground of the world which transcends that world. Thus Nietzsche's concept of eternity cannot be thought as an "attribute" belonging to a traditionally conceived world ground. We say, for instance, that "God is eternal" and mean by this that God *is* always. Here eternity is a "quality" of God's existence, his ever-lasting life. But the concept of a world ground is totally lacking in Nietzsche, so eternity must have another meaning. This meaning must be thought in its relation to the world and to time. Nietzsche's eternity is not transcendent. It relates to the world without coinciding with that world. It is not *eternity of*, but eternal return. Stated in traditional language, it is not a quality belonging to a substance, but rather a unique, sheer "activity."

With reference to this world, to *the* world for Nietzsche, lack of finality means that nothing is ever totally finished. Of course, lack of finality involves a denial of teleology and ultimate goals, but its meaning goes even deeper than this. The very structure of the Will to Power demands temporary goals in order that an increase of power be attained, but these goals are never final. Any final state is absolutely incompatible with the essence of the Will to Power. Just as there can be no final state as the ultimate goal of the world, there can also be no "finished" state, in the sense of a changeless first cause of the world or, for that matter, any first cause at all.

The implications of this lack of finality for an understanding of time (and from this understanding of time, an understanding of eternity) are immense. Instead of conceiving of lack of finality as the impossibility of a first cause or a final goal of the world, let us relate it to time itself. If time is not to be thought as "duration with an 'in vain,'" if it is not to be thought as duration at all, we must consider the moment, the prime "constituent" of time.

What sense does it make to say that the moment has no end? To say that the moment has no end does not mean to say that it is *endless*. This makes no sense. There is no such thing as an endless moment. The statement that the moment has no end means that the moment has no finality in itself. It is precisely this lack of finality of the moment or instant which makes possible (1) instantaneity and (2) the attainment of eternity.

The most important thing about the moment is to think its *arising* and *perishing*. Moments of time are not strung out like a series of atomistic points which may be continuous or discontinuous. Each moment arises and perishes, and it is precisely its perishing or passing away which allows the next moment to arise, to come into being. Thus, in one sense the moment is "endless," in that it reaches no abiding finality in itself but allows the next moment to arise. "In time" nothing is ever completed or finished, but this character of never being finished *breaks through* the concept of "in time" as an absolute framework. The character of never being finished generates a continuous arising, not a continuous, horizontal flux. Thus, moments are not linked together in a horizontal, inevitable causal connection, but can *end*, and this is their relation to eternity. Moments do not end *in time*, because they allow other moments to arise. This is time's quality of having no end. Moments do end, however, because each vanishes. The moment has no abiding "place." It cannot end *in time*. It ends "vertically" into eternity. Eternity is that "dimension" of time into which time ends.

The previous question of the relation of one moment to every moment is a kind of temporal formulation of the question of the relation of the individual (one moment) to the universal (the whole of time). In the light of what has been said about the moment, this relation can be reformulated in terms of time's having no end. Nietzsche's emphasis is not actually on the whole of time, but on *every* moment—that is, on the continual arising of the new moment. The dichotomy between "one" and "every" disappears because it is precisely the "no end" quality of one moment which allows every moment to arise and allows the world to be "the attained release of God in every moment."[10] Thus Nietzsche can speak of the "absolute instantaneity of the Will to Power"[11] and can say that "every power draws its ultimate consequence in every moment."[12] The obscure statement about the "absolute lack of effect of power and causality"[13] suddenly begins to make some

[10] *Birth of Tragedy*, "Attempt at Self-Criticism," 5.
[11] *Nachlass*, XII: 62.
[12] *The Will to Power*, 634.
[13] *Nachlass*, XIV.

sense when it is considered in the light of the instantaneous, endless ending of time. Nietzsche's "causality" in that statement is not a causality which disperses its force into an effect. This causality is power, the More, the culminating, joy as a plus feeling of power.[14]

To repeat, these are ideas that Nietzsche touched on, but whose implications he never developed. Without knowing it, he came very close to a Buddhist theory of time[15] which was apparently never discovered by his "Eastern" mentor Schopenhauer. Schopenhauer was concerned with the cycles of birth, death, and rebirth central to the mythology of early Buddhism and to Brahmanism. Nietzsche somehow gained experience of the instantaneity of time and then partially attempted to reinterpret it in terms of the cycles familiar to him, above all from Schopenhauer.

It is neither possible nor necessary to develop this theory of time completely in order to understand Nietzsche's thought of eternal return. The most basic insight of Nietzsche's thought concerns the non-finality of time, and we shall limit ourselves to the implications of that insight rather than plunge into the intricacies of Buddhism. One might even say that part of Nietzsche's emphasis on eternal return as a *thought* was born of his realization that he had not completely penetrated his own experience. He somehow seemed to know that eternal return was yet to be really *thought out*. Thus he presented it as a doctrine still to be fathomed and was very concerned about the effect it might have, particularly on the higher types of man.

Yet we must at least mention briefly the Buddhist concepts of samsara and nirvana again in this context, for they are central to the problem of "no end." Whereas the West takes an infinity of time (eternity as endless time) to be something desirable and "positive," the East regards an infinity of time (the endlessly recurring cycles of samsara) as something full of suffering and "negative," particularly since a profound ignorance (avidya) is

---

[14] See pp. 80–82.

[15] I am unfortunately unable to give any useful references to this theory in English. I am aware of a theory of instantaneous time in Indian Buddhism (*ksanikatvavada*) and perhaps in Japanese Buddhism (*uji*), but I am not aware of any explication of the *meaning* of these theories. The thoughts developed here are my own.

linked to these cycles. If a Westerner is asked whether he prefers annihilation in death or eternal life, he will probably choose the latter. An Easterner would say (as did Plato with an entirely different emphasis in the *Phaedo*) that there is no annihilation in death. Life follows upon death, just as death follows upon life. Therefore, "eternal life" in the Eastern sense means endlessly recurring world cycles, not some beatific transcendent state. One cannot, so to speak, catapult out of the dimension of birth and death to some other state without a profound transformation of consciousness. Physical death cannot alter that dimension. This profound transformation of consciousness leads to nirvana, the enlightened release from endlessness; yet it *is* at the same time this nirvana. Nirvana is the only way out of unknowing endlessness. There is no "automatic" annihilation in death. Nirvana is not annihilation; it is an enlightened ending.

Nietzsche faced the problem of endlessness in *The Uses and Disadvantages of History for Life*, where he stated that no one would like to live his life over again. The historically oriented man would say "no" because he expects happiness around the corner, in *this* life; another life is not necessary for his goal. The suprahistorically oriented man, however, would say "no" because the world is finished, its end is attained, in every moment.[16]

Endless prolongation is not the "answer" to the question of the meaning of man's life and what he wants of that life. Beyond question and answer, that "meaning" lies in the attainment of an "ending" which is absolutely final, which can never be replaced by something else, partly because it itself has no "place." It cannot be lost, because it is not within the process of endlessness. The process of endlessness cannot touch it, but *it* can transform that process.

TIME

Instead of holding to the characteristics of time mentioned before —the flux and "in time"—we shall now suggest four different characteristics of time which might be more compatible than the

[16] *The Uses and Disadvantages of History for Life* (New York: The Library of Liberal Arts, 1957), 1.

first two with an attempt to understand Nietzsche's thought of eternal return. The four characteristics are: (1) instantaneity, (2) irreversibility, (3) differentiation of the modes of the past, present, and future, and (4) neutrality.

Instantaneity

In contrast to the image of time as a continuous flux, instantaneity emphasizes the "occurrence" of time, the arising, immediate perishing, and arising anew of the instant. This is not the same as a "processual" theory of time or, for that matter, of Being. A processual theory of time takes the flux of time as something ultimate out of which things and events coagulate or are crystallized (Bergson, Whitehead). Instantaneity, on the other hand, simply refers to the occurring of the instant and, through the instantaneous passing away of that instant, to the arising of the next instant. Thus instantaneity does not primarily emphasize the disparate, discontinuous quality of time. This would still be tantamount to a "horizontal" way of thinking, negatively oriented against continuity and duration. Rather, instantaneity means the "vertical" arising and passing away of the instant(s). It is not in itself sufficient for a full-blown theory of time, but it provides, so to speak, the "bare givenness" of time.

It is unfortunate to have to harp so much on the concepts horizontal and vertical. They do not explain very much, for they are primarily "spatial" concepts, as are most of our concrete concepts. They function solely as provisional expedients in the effort to get away from some traditional theories of time.

Irreversibility

The main difficulty about the irreversibility of time lies in thinking it as other than purely directional. Even thought as a direction, time's irreversibility is an incontrovertible fact in all aspects of life —in organic growth, in physical processes such as entropy (time's arrow), and in personal experience. If one is in an unpleasant or painful situation, the irreversibility of time can be a blessing: "this, too, shall pass." If one clings to something in the past which can never again be or to a present situation about to become past, the irreversibility of time means the certain loss of what one has. Of course, this feeling about the irreversibility of time is experienced as the exclusion of the future. In taking things away from us, the irreversibility of time also "brings" new things to us. Yet there is a sense in which we cling to the experienced past or even the experienced present in a way that we never can cling to the future. Anticipation does not cling. If disappointed, it re-anticipates. It has lost nothing, for it has had nothing. It is the past or the present about to become past (that is, the present already *felt* as past) to which we cling, and this clinging itself constitutes the oppressive character of time's irreversibility. Everything is transitory. Nothing remains.

With regard to the irreversibility of time, two things should be said. First, it should be emphasized that it is the clinging to things which constitutes the oppressive character of time's irreversibility. There is in itself nothing oppressive about the normal, irreversible passing of, for instance, a day or a week. Only when one clings to something and thus, so to speak, obstructs the free arising and perishing of the instants of time, is this oppressiveness felt.

Second, one should face the question of how it would be if things did remain just as they are. Even if the static persistence of some situation were possible, the result would probably be horrible. The idea requires acrobatic thinking because it is so unnatural. Given the static persistence of a situation, the situation would probably somehow turn into a caricature of itself because there is no life or presence without occurrence—that is, without the dynamic character of just *becoming* present, which constitutes the intensity of experience. Persistence cannot be experienced. It excludes experience. Thus the wish to hang on to things or situations, the wish that they *remain*, has its perverse element, for it is self-defeating, even self-destructive.

To return to the question of non-directional irreversibility, it must be stated that the irreversibility of time has a meaning far more profound than that of direction. To understand this, we must relate irreversibility to the moment. Again we must ask, In what sense is the moment itself irreversible? If time's irreversibility is not thought as a direction, then the statement that the moment is irreversible does not refer primarily to the fact that it must vanish into the "past." The irreversibility of the moment, or instant, is the reflex of eternity in time. Spatially, irreversibility means that you cannot turn around and go in the opposite direction. Temporally, irreversibility means that what has been cannot be again. Instead of being an irretrievable loss, however, irreversibility can also mean that what "has been" (Nietzsche's "it was") *was* so totally and completely that, not only need it not come again and repeat itself, but also it *could* never repeat itself—it is not in the usual sense past or in any possible sense "in time." The irreversibility of the moment consists in the possibility of its ending into eternity, where nothing is "lost." This will become clearer in the discussion of time and eternity in the last section of this chapter.

Differentiation of the Modes of Past, Present, and Future

If time is thought as instantaneity, then its prime mode is the present, in accordance with the originating character of that mode. Time does not flow out of the future into the past. This concept of time does not explain time's incalculable quality of *presence*, which is admittedly difficult to fathom. The arising of the moment does not really explain presence, but it does after a fashion describe the occurrence of presence.

If time is never extended, even as duration, the past and the future must be thought in the present as the dimensionality of that present. They are what prevents the moment from being a mere atom of time. If the past and the future "are" only in the present, they become "moments" (factors) of the present. They lose the meaning of a non-present present. The past moment is the moment that has just ended, thus allowing the present to originate. The future moment is the moment that is about to originate from the imminent ending of the present. Thus, past, present, and future are close to the simultaneity which constitutes time's dimensionality, the possibility of a kind of "fullness" of time. This simultaneity prevents time from being a mere succession of contracted points bearing no relationship to one another. The modes of time interpenetrate in the moment.

Apart from the characteristic of irreversibility, which cannot be separated from time, the manner of the relationship of the modes of time is not fixed. The future can never be "before" the past, the past can never be "after" the future, but the past can, as in the phenomenon of the "it was," rigidify. Instead of freely ending and allowing the present to arise of itself, the past can persist as a kind of foundation *upon which* the "present" must occur.[17] Then things originate "firmly knotted together," not instantaneously. They occur on the foundation of the "always already there," and all possibility of free origination of the moment is lost.

Similarly, the present can be lost through constant, false expectation. This kind of expectation puts everything off into the future. The future will "bring" this and that; one must wait; it cannot possibly happen *now*. The desired future never comes, however, because such an attitude insists on keeping it always future, in order to *possess* it as untouched possibility. Were the future to become present, it might not be just what was expected. It also would no longer be in the mode of being unriskingly possessed, because one can "possess" only the *expectation* of the future. Once the future becomes present, it has its own reality.

What makes it possible for the modes of time to be related to one another in different ways? There are many other questions with regard to time which belong here—for instance, the great variety in the experience of the "tempo" of time, whether it passes by slowly or quickly. This question is usually pushed aside with the ready "answer" that such an experience of the slow or fast passing of time is purely "subjective" and depends on factors such as moods of boredom, happiness, impatience, keen anticipation, and the like. The fact that one speaks of "subjective," "objective," "psychological," and "aesthetic" time, however, calls for an explanation. If time is presumably one, how can there be so many different "times"? The answer to this question leads us to the final characteristic of time: neutrality.

Neutrality

The literal meaning of the word "neutrality" is "neither," not one thing or the other. Thus, neutrality means a certain indiffer-

[17] See the discussion of the "it was" on pp. 8–13.

ence. With reference to time this means, among other things, that time can never be equated with one of its modes. Above all, it means that there is nothing "prestructured" about time. The "bare givenness" of time is the arising and perishing of the moment, which in itself is not structured, is not a structure, but is the neutral possibility of a structure.

This brings us to the problem of temporal structure. A temporal structure is not a structure "in time." This would be tantamount to falling back on the idea of time as the absolute framework and then trying to create a temporal structure within that framework. Rather, instantaneous time bears within itself the possibility of generating temporal structures, and to be able to do this it must have no (definite) structure.

The question of temporal structure cuts across all the areas of our experience which we have so cleanly separated. Temporal structure is taken here in the broadest possible sense of the *way* in which anything "is" what it is. Thus a tree has a (rather simple) temporal structure—that is, its growth. A drama or a piece of music has a far more complicated temporal structure: its unfolding within an aesthetic context. "Consciousness" has perhaps the most complicated (but not of itself the most organized) temporal structure of all. What differentiates a temporal structure from other kinds of structure is its unfolding quality. It is not present all at once, but constitutes itself in its unfolding. In this unfolding, something "accumulates," and perhaps culminates. For example, thoughts accumulate in a thought process and perhaps culminate in a conclusion.

Neutrality as the possibility of *different* temporal structures implies a certain dimension of "freedom." Here the old philosophical question of the relation of nature to consciousness comes to mind. Nature cannot by itself be anything other than what it is. (For our purposes here we must put aside the vastly complicated question of the profound transformation of nature through man and his "consciousness" into something quite other than it is.) Barring the hungry squirrel, the acorn grows into an oak tree. It cannot choose to grow into anything else or even choose not to grow. The same is more or less true of the animal, who is, as Nietzsche remarks in the second of four essays, *Thoughts Out of Season,*

121

"bound to the stake of the moment." It is not true of man, however, for man is never what he is. He never coincides completely with some preconceived essence or "what," nor does he ever know exactly what he will become.

The problem of the relation of nature to consciousness is, of course, a formidable one. German Idealism in particular grappled with this problem, using all the intricacies of speculative dialectic and thought. Nietzsche could not avoid it in his thought of eternal return, as is evidenced by the way in which he sways back and forth between the two extreme possibilities of deterministic recurrence, on the one hand, and a freedom and a power for man, on the other hand, which far exceeds anything that traditional philosophy has ever imagined, let alone believed. Deterministic recurrence is documented by the statement: "The task is to live in such a way that you must *wish* to live again—you will *in any case*." [18] Perhaps the gaping-asunder of the two extreme possibilities and the glimpse of radical freedom were the "abyss" before which Zarathustra shrank again and again, hesitating and absolutely refusing to speak his "thought," even when he was commanded to do so.[19] The abyss is not so much frightening, although it is that, too. It is above all "abysmal," so much so that no one can think it out to the end. We shall only try to indicate its nature.

The abyss that hovered before Nietzsche's inner eye was the possibility (as opposed to deterministic recurrence) not only of man's becoming free from that recurrence but of his actually transforming it. Not only is "consciousness" an element of freedom in man himself; if "actualized" in the right way, consciousness could extend its dimension of freedom and its power over nature as well.

He should only become conscious of what gives him the highest feeling and shrink before *no means*. It is a matter of *eternity!*[20]

Consciousness, thought of here not as a *cogito* belonging to an ego, both of which Nietzsche rejected, but rather as a unique

[18] *Nachlass* (Kröner ed.), vol. 83, p. 474.
[19] See *Zarathustra*, II, "The Stillest Hour."
[20] *Nachlass* (Kröner ed.), vol. 83, p. 475.

kind of awareness and insight, is capable of attaining tremendous power.

Determinism: I myself am fate and *have conditioned existence for all eternity.*[21]

Still more explicitly, Nietzsche wrote:

As soon as man is *completely humanity, he moves the whole of nature.*[22]

What Nietzsche meant here by "humanity" lies closest to the best of what he meant by his much misunderstood term the "super-man."

If neutrality is a fundamental characteristic of time, this means that there is nothing necessarily given in "the nature of things" to obstruct the realization of this power-full freedom. Nietzsche nowhere gives any concrete indication as to how the relation of nature to consciousness is to be thought. He neither states unequivocally that determined nature is real, consciousness being a non-essential, inefficacious part of it, nor that consciousness is real, nature being illusory in the strict determinacy of its causal laws (veil of Maya or illusion). He only points to the possibility that there is no inherent obstruction to freedom in the nature of things.

TIME AND ETERNITY IN THE ETERNAL RETURN OF THE SAME

In the light of the four characteristics of time just discussed, time can be defined generally as what has no end, as what happens again and again, is never finished and ultimate. Eternity we shall define as the Ultimate.

Eternity as the Ultimate is indeed a kind of "absolute" in the bare meaning of that word of being "released" from the world. But if eternity as the Ultimate is a kind of *temporal* absolute, many of the traditional qualifications of the Absolute will not fit it. Anselm, for instance, defined God as that than which nothing

[21] *Ibid.*, pp. 488 and 499.
[22] *Ibid.*, p. 487.

greater can be thought. In contrast to Descartes, who subsequently turned Anselm's "than which nothing greater can be thought" into the highest being, Anselm preserved the element of absolute transcendence of God. Whereas for Descartes God is the highest being reached by thought, for Anselm God is always still beyond thought, no matter how far thought transcends the world. One could formulate Anselm's idea in a more general fashion and say that God is that which thought cannot go beyond, which implies also that thought cannot actually attain God, for what has been attained is at the same time in a certain sense transcended.

Transferring the general formulation of Anselm's argument to the setting of Nietzsche's thought, that beyond which it is impossible to go (an expression of the highest transcendence) might become that after which nothing more can come: the Ultimate. How do these two expressions differ? First of all, the second phrase lacks an explicit emphasis on thought. This is in keeping with Nietzsche's rejection of the *cogito* (and thus indirectly of Anselm's *quo maius* cogitari *nihil possit*) and his avoidance of the later development of that *cogito* as transcendental reflection. Second, "unable to go beyond" (in thought) becomes: "nothing more can come." The first phrase expresses the absolute limit of transcendence. The second phrase expresses the absolute ending of occurrence.

The shift from the first to the second phrase represents the difference between the transcending movement of thought (going beyond finite things) and the ending movement of time as sheer occurrence encompassing possibilities of thought and "being." What is the difference between transcending and ending? Transcendence "climbs over" things, leaving them behind in order to approach something which it can no longer transcend. Standing on the foundation of transcended finite things, thought stops short before an absolute limit which it cannot transcend.

Ending is the self-release of the moment. It is not an end or a limit which must be transcended. An end or a limit closes something off, sets its boundaries, and gives it a self-containedness which cannot be broken out of. Ending as the self-release of the moment neither closes something off nor leaves anything behind, but rather allows things to be. Only the self-release of the moment makes the unobstructed being of things possible. "Transcendence" of the moment of time thus makes no sense and is furthermore impossible, because the instantaneous moment does not persist long enough to be transcended. In its self-release the moment accomplishes its own "transcendence," its ending into eternity. When related to instantaneous time, expressions for the transcendence of time, "timeless" and particularly "out of time," have little meaning. They are meaningful only in relation to durational time.

In what sense is eternity the absolute ending of occurrence? It is not so in the sense that it is cessation. Eternity is rather that in which occurrence ends. If occurrence or time ends into eternity, nothing is "left over" which would necessitate further occurrence or repetition (recurrence) in the broad sense. When, for instance, does one continue or repeat an action? When the action is not finished, when it has not attained what it was intended to accomplish, when it is imperfect. This is most evident in the realm of "practice," in which our lives largely consist, whether this be the practice of thinking, of art, or of living itself. "Practice makes perfect." When practice attains its end, the activity is per-fect —that is, accomplished to the end. Nothing remains or is left over which was not attained, and thus no further repetition or activity is required. Repetition in the fruitful sense of practice becomes, once the practice of a particular activity is perfected, a meaningless, deadening activity if it is blindly continued. It can distort what has already been acquired or reached. Further activity in this case would be an inability to stop.

In eternity a finality is attained which we normally associate only with the past. What is past cannot be changed. It has already happened. It is final. The finality that we know is reached only at the price of something being "over" and gone. The condition of that finality is the *absence* of something. Were it yet present, it could still change. Eternity, however, can never be past, because it is never "in time." Eternity preserves this element of finality *in presence*.

Thus eternity is not changeless in the sense of a static persistence having nothing to do with time or occurrence. Eternity is "changeless" only in the sense that what is attained there can never be lost or dispersed, because nothing can come after it. It is not so much

125

that eternity "breaks into" time as that time "breaks out into" eternity. Eternity can never be "in time." It is neither in time nor out of time in the sense of being the changeless which excludes time. Eternity is not the changeless absolute, but rather the absolving (*ab-solvere*) of time.

The relation of time to eternity is not one of opposition (nor of opposition in the sense of overcoming or transcendence) at all. What is opposed must persist to form that opposition, and neither time *nor* eternity does this. Time cannot, because of its instantaneous again and again. Eternity does not, because of its absolved never again. The *basis* for opposition is never built up. Eternity is not the "goal" of time in the sense that it could be attained by a directed process. Instantaneous time lacks the continuity to build up such a cumulative process. It does not accumulate processually. It culminates into the extreme ultimate.

In conclusion, let us relate these remarks specifically to an interpretation of Nietzsche's thought of eternal return. Return is the movement of time into eternity, constituting the Same in the sense that there is *ultimately* no discrepancy between time and eternity. Because there is no discrepancy, nothing is left over which has to recur. The word "eternal" in this thought then refers not to a changeless absolute but to time itself in the inexhaustibility of its again and again ending into eternity.

A final word about the meaning of the word "Same" (*das Gleiche*). The word "same" expresses some kind of identity. A thing is the same as itself. A person retains a certain personal identity throughout his life. We stated earlier that to understand the word "same" in relation to eternal return makes of the Same a content caught in the form of recurring time cycles. Given uniform, absolute recurring cycles, the whole emphasis of meaning is placed upon the content, upon *what* recurs.

At the end of the "Amphiboly of the Concepts of Reflection" in the *Critique of Pure Reason*, Kant singles out the concepts of form and matter or content and states that they lie at the foundation of all other reflection, so inseparably are they connected with every mode of exercising the understanding. Kant's emphasis is, of course, on form as the forms of our experiencing and on matter as what is "given" to those forms to be synthesized, but the concepts

themselves undoubtedly extend beyond Kant's specific epistemological emphasis.

Thus, if time is not thought as a form in which things occur
(or, here, recur), "what" occurs in eternal return should not be
thought as the content of this form. If "what" occurs in eternal
return is not a content, the kind of "identity" to be thought in
Nietzsche's word "the Same" refers neither to the self-identity of
things or persons nor even, strictly speaking, to some kind of
"identity" between time and eternity in the sense that individual,
successive moments of time are subsumed under the simultaneous
whole of eternity. At best, the "identity" of time and eternity could
be expressed by saying that time is as-*simil*-ated to eternity. The
Same is this *process of as-simil-ation,* a manner of occurring which
first determines *any* possible "what," any thing or person or whatever. Thus the question with regard to the Same is not What is
it that comes again? Rather, if one asks, as one must, about what
it is that comes again, one must first ask about the manner in
which the "what" is constituted by the "how." The "how" in this
case is not the inexorable form of time, but the power-full freedom of possibilities of being.

One is an artist at the price of experiencing that which all non-
artists call "form" as *content,* as "the thing itself." Then one of course
belongs to a *transformed world,* for from then on content becomes
something merely formal, our life included.[23]

[23] *The Will to Power,* 818.

SELECTED
BIBLIOGRAPHY

For a complete bibliography up to 1960, see *International Nietzsche Bibliography*, edited by H. W. Reichert and K. Schlechta (Chapel Hill: University of North Carolina Press, 1960).

Ackermann, Manfred. "Das Kreissymbol im Werk Nietzsches." Dissertation. Munich, 1968.

Barthel, Ernst. "Nietzsches Lehre vom Ring der Zeit und ihre gegenwärtige Fortbildung." *Bayreuther Blätter*, 59 (1936).

Bueb, Bernhard. *Nietzsches Kritik der praktischen Vernunft*. Stuttgart: Ernst Klett Verlag, 1970.

Buri, Fritz. *Kreuz und Ring*. Bern, 1947.

Collins, James. *The Existentialists: A Critical Study*. Chicago: Henry Regnery Co., 1952.

Danto, A. *Nietzsche as Philosopher*. New York: Macmillan Co., 1965.

Eliade, Mircea. *Le mythe de l'éternel retour*. Paris, 1949.

Ewald, Oskar. *Nietzsches Lehre in ihren Grundbegriffen*. Berlin, 1903.

Fink, Eugen. *Nietzsches Philosophie*. Stuttgart: Kohlhammer Verlag, 1960.

Gaultier, Jules de. "Nietzsche et l'idee du retour éternel." *Mercure de France*, 227 (1931).

Granier, Jean. *Le problème de la Vérité dans la philosophie de Nietzsche*. Paris: Editions du Seuil.

Gutmann, James. "The Tremendous Moment." *Journal of Philosophy*, 51 (1954).

Halévy, Daniel. "Le travail de Zarathustra." *Paris*, 1909.

Heidegger, Martin. *Nietzsche.* Pfullingen: Neske Verlag, 1961.
———. "Nietzsches Wort 'Gott ist Tot.'" in *Holzwege.* Frankfurt: Klostermann Verlag, 1952.
———. *What Is Called Thinking?* New York: Harper & Row, 1968.
———. "Who Is Nietzsche's Zarathustra?" *Review of Metaphysics,* March, 1967.
Hester, R. *Eternal Recurrence.* La Salle, Ill.: Open Court Publishing Co., 1932.
Jaspers, Karl. *Nietzsche: An Introduction to the Understanding of His Philosophical Activity.* Translated by C. F. Wallraff and F. J. Schmitz. Tucson: University of Arizona Press, 1969.
Kaufmann, Walter. *Nietzsche: Philosopher, Psychologist, Antichrist.* 3rd ed. Princeton: Princeton University Press, 1950.
Löwith, Karl. "Nietzsche's Doctrine of Eternal Recurrence." *Journal of the History of Ideas,* 6 (1945).
———. *Nietzsches Philosophie der ewigen Wiederkunft.* Stuttgart, 1956.
Marchal, Robert. "Le retour éternel." *Archives de philosophie,* 3 (1925).
Rey, Abel. *Le retour éternel et la philosophie de la physique.* Paris, 1927.
Riboni, Denise. "Nietzsche et l'idée du retour éternel." *Suisse contemporaine,* 4 (1944).
Stambaugh, Joan. "Das Problem des Gleichen in Nietzsches Gedanken der ewigen Wiederkunft des Gleichen." *Revue de philosophie,* 1964.
———. *Untersuchungen zum Problem der Zeit bei Nietzsche.* The Hague: Martinus Nijhoff, 1959.
Stohmann, Walter. *Überblick über die Geschichte des Gedankens der ewigen Wiederkunft.* Munich, 1917.
Struve, Wolfgang. *Die neuzeitliche Philosophie als Metaphysik der Subjektivität.* N.p. 1949.
Tschizewskij, Dmylro. *Dostojewski und Nietzsche: Die Lehre von der ewigen Wiederkunft.* Bonn, 1947.

INDEX

Anselm, 123–24
Aristotle, 22, 34
Art, 82–86, 88; and Will to
    Power, 98, 99
Augustine, 22

Becoming, 4, 13, 14, 47; and art,
    83–84; cycles of, 34; and the
    death of God, 90, 92–93; as
    self-justification, 100–101. *See
    also* Innocence of Becoming
Being, 1, 3, 13, 44, 108; and art,
    83–84; and the death of God,
    90–92; possibilities of, 4, 127;
    rejection of, by Nietzsche, 70–
    71; as what is real, 75
Berkeley, George, 63
Birth of Tragedy, The, 83, 84–85
Brahmanism, 5, 23
Buddhism, xv–xvi; cycles in, 115–
    16; Hinayana, 5; Nietzsche's
    affinity to, 18. *See also* Nihil-
    ism, as European form of
    Buddhism

Christianity, 2, 90, 97
Christian morality, 98
Circle, 36–38, 39, 52, 54, 107
Consciousness, 9, 121–23
Contradiction, principle of, 20
Cycles, 9, 103; in Buddhism,
    115–16; recurrence of, xii, 23,
    34, 105, 107, 126

Darwin, Charles, 88
Darwinism, 5, 23, 82
Descartes, René, 34, 63, 74, 124
Duration, 6–8, 26; as endless in-
    difference, 3, 32–33, 34, 109,
    110–11

Ecce Homo, 4, 104
Empiricists, 76–77
Eternal present (*nunc stans*), 6,
    25; as concept of eternity, 3,
    111
Eternity: as activity, 113; as an
    "always," 20–21; as connected
    with the idea of substance, 7–

8; definition of, 123–27; as endlessness, 3–4; four basic conceptions of, 109–12; as immanence, 3; its relationship to time, 3, 5–8, 9; and moment, 24–25; as return of the same, 3–4; as traditionally thought, 1, 3; as vertical dimension, 106–7, 114

Fatalism, 32, 56, 59
Fate, 56–59
Fichte, J. G., 62
Finality, lack of, xvi, 93–94, 112–16; and the idea of no end, 3–4, 34, 45, 47, 50–51
Finitude, 4, 12, 13, 33
Force, 45–49, 81; and power, 52–53

Genealogy of Morals, The, 7, 79, 82
German Idealism, 122. *See also* Fichte; Hegel
God, 1, 3, 4, 17, 35; Anselm's concept of, 123–24; and the concept of power, 19–20, 99–101; death of, 88, 90–94; Descartes' concept of, 124; as eternal, in every moment, 113, 114

Hegel, G. W. F.: absolute subject of, 62, 63, 65–69; concept of eternity as simultaneity, 111–12; concept of time in, 68–69, 104
Heidegger, Martin: on Nietzsche

as last metaphysical figure, 14, 94, 96–97
Heraclitus: kinship of, with Nietzsche, 26, 85
Hume, David: on the self as a bundle of impressions, 61, 63, 64, 77

Immanence, 91
Innocence of Becoming: as the most basic fact of existence, 87, 91–94; as sheer occurrence, 108
Instant. *See* Moment; Plato
Instantaneity, 113; as a characteristic of time, 117
Irreversibility, time as, 8–9, 40–41, 117–19
"It was," as a hindrance to eternal return, 8, 10–13

Joy, 16, 81; Dionysian, 84, 101–2
Joyful Wisdom, The, 56

Kant, Immanuel, xiv; form and matter in, 126–27; his concept of the self, 63, 64–65, 74–75; and time, 64, 68; universal subjectivity of, 76

Leibniz, G. W. F., 6
Locke, John, 63

Man. *See* Fate
Mechanism, rejected by Nietzsche, 47, 48–51
Meister Eckhart, 9n15

Modes of time, 119–20
Moment: as contradiction of past and future, 37–41; enigmatic character of, 21–27; and finality, 113–15; as related to the Moment, 107–8; self-release of, 124–25

Nachlass, 23, 33, 41, 87, 89, 95; discussion of physics in, 45, 51; discussion of self in, 70, 72
Neutrality, time as, 33–34, 120–23
Newton, I., 62
Nihilism, xii, 1, 32; as European form of Buddhism, 17–19, 21, 34, 103
Now. *See* Aristotle; Moment

Occam's razor, 7

Pantheism, 17, 91; of Nietzsche, 19, 101
Physics, xiii; and the idea of no end, 45, 47, 50–51
Positivism, 75–76
Power, 19–20, 46, 52–54; as related to will, 79–80, 97–102
Plato, xii, 2, 21–22
Platonism, 50–51
Pythagoreans, xii

Recurrence: etymology of, 29–31; nihilistic form of, 5, 54–55
Repetition, 105, 125
Return: etymology of, 29–31
Revenge, 13, 93; as ontological concept, 10–13; redemption from, 108

Same, 16, 26, 102; attainment of, in every moment, 17, 18, 21; etymology of, 31; meaning of, 126–27; as movement, 107–8; problem of, 31–33, 71–76; return of, 3, 13, 14, 30, 61; self as, 61–62
Schelling, F. W. J., 97
Schopenhauer, Arthur, 115; Nietzsche's criticism of, 4, 7, 9n, 14, 15, 77–79; negative nature of will in, 97–99
Self, 59, 81; as behavioristically determined events, 61–62; as idealistically structured subject, 61–62; problem of, 71–76; the Same as, 61–62; traditional theory of, 63–69, 73; and will, 77–80
Simultaneity: as concept of eternity, 3, 109, 111–12
Space, 8–9, 21; in Hegel, 67–68; spatial as distinguished from temporal, 39–40
Spinoza, B., 91
Subject-object split, and Nietzsche's interpretation of eternal return, 34–35, 50
Suffering, 36, 54; as ontological concept, 12, 18
Superman, 23, 54; as the goal of man, 88–90; problem of, 81–82, 86

Technology, xiii
Teleology, rejection of, 21, 26, 107, 108, 113

Temporal structures, problem of, 121–22

Thoughts Out of Season, 82, 121

Time, 4, 7, 24, 38, 107; characteristics of, 109–12, 116–23; definition of, 123; and duration, 6–8, 33; and eternity, 5–8, 20–21, 126–27; Hegel and, 68–69; infinite nature of, 45–47; irreversibility of, 8–9, 40–41, 117–19; its relationship to lack of finality, 113–16; Kant and, 64, 68; neutrality of, 33–34, 120–23; traditional theories of, 104–5

Timelessness, 3, 109, 112

Transcendence, 1, 91; and lack of finality, 112–13, 124–25

Transmigration, xii, xiii, 5

Transvaluation, of all values, xv, 55

"True World," as fable, 2

Uses and Disadvantages of History for Life, The, 87, 116

Value, 1–2; concept of, in Nietzsche, xv, 55, 98

"Vision and enigma," in the thought of eternal return, 35–45

Western dualism, xiii

Will: and eternal return, 96–99; revenge and, 10–12; and the self, 77–80; and the Will to Power, 10–12, 77

Will to More, 13–16, 19–20, 80–81

Will to Power, xv, 53, 55, 89, 90, 91; as art, 82–86; as basis for the self, 81–82; and eternal return, 77, 94–102; as lack of finality, 113–14; as rejection of mechanism, 48–49; and revenge, 10–13; the will and, 77–80; as a Will to More, 13–16, 80–81

Will to Power, 13, 57, 106

Zarathustra, 5, 9, 54, 92, 106; eternal return in, xii–xiii, 16, 70; superman in, 82, 86, 88; "vision and enigma" in, 35–45